P9-CQI-258

THE LEADERSHIP LIBRARY
VOLUME 15
THE MAGNETIC FELLOWSHIP

Other books in THE LEADERSHIP LIBRARY

Well-Intentioned Dragons by Marshall Shelley

Liberating the Leader's Prayer Life by Terry Muck

Clergy Couples in Crisis by Dean Merrill

When It's Time to Move by Paul D. Robbins, ed.

Learning to Lead by Fred Smith

What Every Pastor Needs to Know about Music, Youth, and Education
  by Garth Bolinder, Tom McKee, and John Cionca

Helping Those Who Don't Want Help by Marshall Shelley

Preaching to Convince by James D. Berkley, ed.

When to Take a Risk by Terry Muck

Weddings, Funerals, and Special Events
  by Eugene Peterson, Calvin Miller, and others

Making the Most of Mistakes by James D. Berkley

Leaders by Harold Myra, ed.

Being Holy, Being Human by Jay Kesler

Secrets of Staying Power by Kevin A. Miller

THE LEADERSHIP LIBRARY

Volume

15

The Magnetic Fellowship

Reaching and Keeping People

Larry K. Weeden, ed.

Carol Stream, Illinois

WORD BOOKS
PUBLISHER
WACO, TEXAS

WORD, CANADA
RICHMOND, B.C.

THE MAGNETIC FELLOWSHIP

Introduction and ancillary copy ©1988 Christianity Today, Inc.

Chapter 1 ©1981 C. Peter Wagner
Chapter 2 ©1984 Donald Gerig
Chapter 3 ©1986 Gary Harrison
Chapter 4 ©1985 Rebecca Pippert
Chapter 5 ©1984 Kenneth Vetters and Cindy Vetters Lanning
Chapter 6 ©1984 Christianity Today, Inc.
Chapter 7 ©1984 Marilyn Kunz
Chapter 8 ©1984 Win Arn and Charles Arn
Chapter 9, part 1 ©1987 Dean Merrill
Chapter 9, part 2 ©1987 E. Stanley Ott
Chapter 10 ©1986 Don M. McDonald
Chapter 11 ©1987 John Cionca
Chapter 12 ©1987 John Savage
Chapter 13 ©1988 Virginia Vagt

A LEADERSHIP/Word Book. Copublished by Christianity Today, Inc. and Word, Inc. Distributed by Word Books.

Cover art by Joe Van Severen.

Library of Congress Cataloging-in-Publication Data

The Magnetic Fellowship.

(The Leadership library ; v. 15)
1. Evangelistic work. 2. Church growth. I. Weeden, Larry K. II. Series.
BV3790.M29 1988 253 88-10674
ISBN 0-917463-20-X

Printed in the United States of America

To Beth,
whose love sustains me

C O N T E N T S

INTRODUCTION

Therefore go and make disciples of all nations.

MATTHEW 28:19

All of us who love the Lord are challenged by the Great Commission. We are commanded to go and make disciples, and out of love we go willingly. Yet despite our best intentions and efforts, many of us are frustrated that our churches are not reaching people as effectively as we'd like.

How can we do a better job of evangelizing? What would make our churches more appealing to visitors? Where can we find ways to more effectively present the gospel?

Just as frustrating as a lack of effective outreach can be the loss of people out the church's back door. Even if new members are coming into the fellowship, there's an inevitable sense of loss and discouragement when others slip away. We lose the opportunity to minister to those individuals and families. We lose workers from the church's ministry. We lose friends from the fellowship. And rightly or wrongly, pastors usually find themselves asking, *What have I done wrong to make them want to leave?*

How can we better meet the needs of those who are drifting away? What can we do differently to rekindle and maintain their enthusiasm for the church's ministry?

The Magnetic Fellowship provides practical answers to these twin concerns of reaching people and transforming them into active, growing disciples. It draws on the contributions of fourteen of LEADERSHIP Journal's best writers. Indeed, three of the chapters, by Becky Pippert, John Savage, and Win and Charles Arn, are among the highest-rated articles (by readers) in the journal's history.

The book follows a progression in addressing these concerns. In part 1 are three chapters that look at what kind of church climate is attractive to visitors and thus conducive to growth. Part 2 has four chapters that explore specific, effective methods of outreach, including personal evangelism and home visitation. The three chapters in part 3 then discuss how best to meet the needs of newcomers, drawing them into the church and helping them grow into committed disciples. And finally, in part 4 are three chapters examining how to keep people involved in church life and active in ministry.

As one pastor, Wayne Jacobsen, once said, "Obedience is our only motivation, and nothing as trivial as size can ever measure it." Certainly that must be our underlying attitude when it comes to carrying out the Great Commission; we don't seek to reach and keep people in the local church for the sake of impressive numbers. Yet we all want to be the best possible stewards of the opportunities God has given us, to be as effective as we can be in carrying out his command. That's the spirit with which we offer *The Magnetic Fellowship*.

— Larry K. Weeden
Associate Editor, LEADERSHIP

O N E

TRAITS OF AN ATTRACTIVE CHURCH

A leader is a dealer in hope.

Napoleon Bonaparte

There are different kinds of gifts, but the same Spirit. . . . Now to each one the manifestation of the Spirit is given for the common good.

1 Corinthians 12:4, 7

Who doesn't look in the mirror and ask, "Am I attractive?" And what pastor doesn't wonder about his or her church, "Are we attractive? What makes a church appealing to new people? What do the truly effective churches have that mine doesn't?"

Few people have worked as hard as C. Peter Wagner to discover the characteristics of churches that do a good job of attracting and meeting the needs of new members. A professor of church growth at Fuller Theological Seminary in Pasadena, California, Wagner explains those traits and shows us how we can make them work in our own situations.

Why lead a church?

Experienced church leaders give different answers to this question. Most of the answers are sincere, and few can really be called bad. "To glorify God" should be and usually is the preamble. But more specifically, some lead a church to promote an outstanding Christian worship experience. Some lead to develop meaningful ties among Christians. Some lead to contribute to the social welfare of the surrounding community. Some lead to teach the Bible to believers. The list could go on and on. In most cases, specific goals of leadership combine several of the above in differing proportions.

But let's focus on yet another purpose of church leadership, namely, church growth. In a broad sense, church growth means improving the quality of the Christian life of the existing members; but it's also concerned with a regular and sustained increase in the number of those members. I hope to clarify some ways church leadership directly relates to the quality attributed to the early church in Jerusalem, where "every day the Lord added to their group those who were being saved" (Acts 2:47, GNB).

Vital Signs of a Church

A few years ago, I wrote a book called *Your Church Can Grow*. I had examined as many anglo-American churches as I could that were sustaining a vigorous growth rate. Since I believe church growth (with some exceptions) is a sign of church health, I identified the growth principles they had in common, calling them "vital signs." They are:

1. A pastor who is a possibility thinker and whose dynamic leadership has been used to catalyze the entire church into action for growth.

2. A well-mobilized laity, which has discovered, has developed, and is using all the spiritual gifts for growth.

3. A church big enough to provide the range of services that meet the expectations of its members.

4. The proper balance of the dynamic relationship between celebration, congregation, and cell.

5. A membership drawn primarily from one homogeneous unit.

6. Evangelistic methods that have been proved to make disciples.

7. Priorities arranged in biblical order.

At least three large tests have been made of the seven vital signs, the latest a computer-based survey of Baptist churches in Great Britain by Paul Beasley-Murray. The feedback has consistently confirmed and strengthened the first two vital signs, those that touch the roles of the pastor and the people in the growth of the church. If I were to write a book now, I would add some things, I would subtract some, and I would say some things differently.

Therefore, I am increasingly convinced that the two indispensible preconditions to vigorous, sustained church growth are a pastor who wants the church to grow and a congregation of people who want the church to grow — and both are willing to pay the price.

What is the price? One price the pastor must pay is a willingness to assume a strong leadership role. One price the people must pay is a willingness to follow growth leadership. How can this happen in a harmonious and dynamic way?

Pastoral Dilemmas

A pastor who conscientiously attempts to serve God in a biblical way is faced with two dilemmas: the relationship of power to humility, and the relationship of leadership to servanthood.

Romans 12:3 teaches humility: "Do not think of yourself more highly than you should." Jesus relates that humility to power when he says, "Whoever makes himself great will be humbled, and whoever humbles himself will be made great" (Matt. 23:12). Notice the two active verbs and the two passive verbs. A pastor can either make an effort to be great or make an effort to be humble. If the latter, God will then make the pastor great. All God-given leadership is rooted in humility. But when the process is complete, the pastor must humbly recognize that he is great. Biblically, power and humility go together.

So do leadership and servanthood. Jesus put them together as a result of the tiff caused among the apostles when James and John requested privileged status in the kingdom. In explanation, Jesus contrasted the heathen rulers and their tyrannical style with Christian rulers who are essentially servants. "If one of you wants to be great, he must be the servant of the rest" (Mark 10:43). The Christian leader must be perceived, by those who follow, as a bona fide servant. There is no other way. Jesus washed the disciples' feet, but while he was doing it, there was no doubt in any of their minds that he was their leader.

Thus, a pastor is a humble servant. But the more humble and the more of a servant, the more leadership and authority is granted by God. And if God grants the authority, it ought to be exercised.

Ranges of Leadership Styles

The way leadership is exercised in a given parish will depend on at least four important sets of factors. Each one of the four will impose outward limits, or ranges, on appropriate leadership styles.

1. Cultural ranges. Built into the fabric of different cultures is a certain range of leadership expectations. In many Latin American situations, for example, a *caudillo* (politically a "strong man") type of leadership is well received. This kind of leadership would be highly inappropriate, however, in an African village, where the cultural decision-making pattern is total consensus. In England, the traditional monarchy seems good to the people, so the Anglican church is ruled by bishops and archbishops. Most Americans, on the other hand, prefer democratic leadership where a vote is taken and the majority opinion prevails. In every culture there is both strong and weak leadership, even though the styles may differ greatly.

2. Socio-economic ranges. In America, members of trade unions respond to a different style of leadership than do business executives and professionals. Christian blue-collar workers tend to thrive in their service to God under fairly directive leadership, while professionals are more comfortable with leadership that allows them to participate more in the decision-making process. My church (Lake Avenue Congregational Church, Pasadena, California) happens to be upper middle class socio-economically. As a result, one of our major pieces of equipment is a huge Xerox machine that collates the printed pages. We need a twelve-page report to change the draperies in the nursery! But Xeroxes and twelve-page reports are altogether superfluous in many other churches, even for such major decisions as calling new staff members.

3. Denominational ranges. Presbyterians in Scotland became fed up with bishops, so they developed an organizational system that would forever exclude that form of leadership. Ruling elders and teaching elders form a session, which

leads the church. Methodists split off from the Anglicans but kept the bishops. The bishop, not the congregation, has the power to remove or assign pastors. Baptists have room for a wide range of styles, from strictly congregational governments to bishoplike pastoral authority in some churches. Each denomination has developed its own leadership traditions, which place limitations on the options of pastors who happen to be serving them.

4. Personality ranges. Each individual also has certain personality traits that limit leadership styles. Some people by nature are take-charge individuals. Strong leadership comes intuitively, and they have little patience for involving others in the decision-making process. For others, a nondirective style feels better. Church leaders need to be aware of their own personalities and temperaments in a realistic way. Moving outside those boundaries may seem to work for a while, but it will usually break down over the long haul.

Leadership and Growth Potential

What pastoral leadership roles contribute to church growth? I can best describe them using a split-image spectrum (Fig. 1).

Notice, first of all, that as we move toward the left, the pastor does most of the leading, and toward the right, the congregation does most of the leading. Research has indicated that the potential for church growth increases as the leadership role of the pastor increases and the leadership role of the congregation decreases.

Very few cultural, socio-economic, denominational, or personality restrictions will allow a pastor to move clear to the left. But a pastor toward the left end of the range will have a better growth situation than one toward the right, other things being equal.

A growing church that very nearly fits the left end of the model (none will fit it in every respect) is the Crystal Cathedral Community Church in California. For more than ten years I

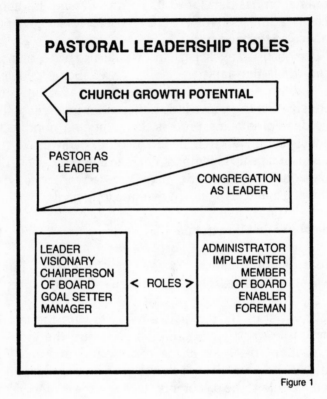

Figure 1

have been observing the growth of that church, which at the time of this writing includes over 5,000 families, or slightly over 10,000 members, with a morning attendance running around 8,000. How did this church, a member of a mainline denomination, the Reformed Church in America, sustain such a dramatic growth rate over twenty-five years?

Quite simply, its pastor, Robert Schuller, functions in the traditional, Reformed Church pastoral role as chairman of the consistory, or board, with all the leadership authority that carries with it. Several years ago, a leadership crisis came at a time when a decision had to be made to purchase the property where the church, with the new Crystal Cathedral, is now located. The two-year struggle ended up with new members of the consistory, who recognized that God had given gifts of faith and leadership to Bob Schuller, and that God's will could best be done if Schuller functioned as a leader with authority. Although church growth is complex, and Schuller's leadership is only one of many growth factors active in this church, it is safe to say that if a new pastor instead of a new consistory had been brought in years ago, the growth pattern would have been considerably less.

As you examine your position on the leadership spectrum, keep in mind the several pairs of labels opposite each other, check the trends, and try to formulate a reasonably accurate profile for yourself.

• The church has a higher potential for growth if the pastor is a leader more than he is an administrator. A leader, as the next pair of labels indicates, is a visionary, whereas an administrator is an implementer of someone else's vision.

• A church growth pastor is a goal-setter; less growth potential is predicted for a pastor with the self-image of an "enabler" who encourages the lay people to set the goals.

• To use an industrial model, the pastor who tends to be more a manager type than a foreman type will enhance the growth possibilities for the church.

Some, at first glance, will object to this, especially pastors who are currently in the thirty- to forty-year age bracket.

When they were in seminary in the sixties and early seventies, the "enabler" was set forth as an ideal role for pastors. But as Lyle Schaller points out in his book *Effective Church Planning*, this frequently turned out to be a counterproductive model. An equipper should not be equated with an enabler if an enabler, by definition, abdicates the responsibility of the top leadership position in the congregation.

Leadership in the New Testament

It seems to me that where the Bible touches on the matter of Christian leadership, it supports the strong leadership role for the pastor. Three Greek words for this role are fairly interchangeable in the New Testament: shepherd or pastor (*poimen*), elder (*presbyteros*), and bishop (*episkopos*). The bishop is an overseer or a guardian. The elder is respected because of the wisdom of age and is a ruler. The relationship of a shepherd to a flock of sheep is one of the biblical metaphors used to describe God-ordained Christian leadership. A pastor, by definition, is related to a flock as its leader.

More specifically, in the several passages where the New Testament deals with the matter of leadership, some highly descriptive and appropriate language is used:

1. John 10:1–5. The pastor shepherds, calls by name, leads, and walks ahead. The people hear his voice, recognize it, and follow him.

2. 1 Thessalonians 5:12–13. The pastor works hard, admonishes, and warns. The people honor, think highly of, and love the pastor.

3. Hebrews 13:17. The pastor has rule, watches over souls, and gives account. The people obey and submit.

4. 1 Peter 5:1–5. The pastor feeds the flock, takes oversight, is an example, and is not a tyrant. The people follow.

Sources of Leadership

If the leadership responsibility of the pastor is so evident in biblical perspective, it might be well to ask where leadership comes from. If a person wants to lead a church, how does this happen? Leadership in the body of Christ is acquired in three major ways:

1. *Leadership is earned.* The leader must be perceived by the followers as their servant, and this is not accomplished overnight. It takes years for people to develop the love and respect for their pastor necessary to open the door for growth leadership. Lyle Schaller says that the effective years of a pastorate *begin* between years four and six. The most obvious exception is the founding pastor of a new congregation, where the full leadership role can begin immediately.

2. *Leadership is developed.* Good training can increase the ability to lead in almost any person motivated to take it. Unfortunately, leadership training has not been a prominent part of ministerial courses in most seminaries and Bible schools, at least until recently. But an increasing number of management seminars are becoming available in continuing education and doctor of ministry programs to help fill this need.

3. *Leadership is a gift.* Although training can help, it can take a person only so far. I hesitate to mention it, because I would not want to discourage anyone from assuming strong pastoral leadership, but leadership is mentioned as one of the spiritual gifts, the *charismata* (Rom. 12:8). As I continue to study large, growing churches, I find there are only two of the spiritual gifts common to all superchurch pastors I know: the gifts of leadership and faith. Since faith is the goal-setting gift, they go together.

Lay Ministry Is the Key

The second vital sign of a healthy church is a well-mobilized laity. By that, however, I do not mean that the congregation should attempt to assume the leadership of the church.

I realize that in many churches, especially those with an attendance at worship of 200 and under (about 85 percent of America's Protestant churches), the congregation, as a matter of fact, does lead the church. Some of them change their pastors so frequently that there is no way a pastor could earn the love and respect of the people as their leader, even if he or she were so inclined. Very few such churches are "adding daily to their number such as should be saved." One of the problems is that they are led by ecclesiastical amateurs. Good-hearted people, yes; saints of God, yes; intelligent and generous and trustworthy, yes; but professional church leaders, no.

Having said this, let me reiterate that lay people need to be active and enthusiastic and wholehearted in their service to God and the church. But their activity needs to be concentrated on *ministry* functions rather than *leadership* functions. This is a crucial point, for little current writing on church leadership makes sufficient distinction between leadership roles and ministry roles. When the two are properly distinguished, strong church leadership can be maintained, avoiding at the same time the ever-present danger of clericalism.

Although Robert Schuller exercises strong, pastoral leadership functions, the people in the church in no way feel tyrannized, oppressed, unfulfilled, or limited in their service to God. In fact, I know of very few churches with a higher level of enthusiastic lay involvement. Schuller has developed a clear philosophy of ministry:

● To reach the unchurched in the area with the message of Jesus Christ.

● To equip those reached to be fully Christian in every aspect of their lives.

● To develop a caring community of believers for spiritual nurture.

● To develop the necessary lay ministry leadership to keep the cycle going.

The first, which is the most directly related to church growth, will not happen without strong programs in the other three.

To accomplish these objectives, Schuller has gathered around him a highly competent, professional staff of ministers. They have broad authority to develop their assigned spheres of ministry. The Lay Ministers Training Center has a

Bible-school-level curriculum of 250 classroom hours covering biblical studies, theology, church history, pastoral care, and other courses. As of this writing, 1,280 persons are actively enrolled in this study program, and a total of 72 have graduated from it and are recognized as "credentialed lay ministers." Few churches have such a reservoir of lay people who have taken that much formal study.

Some 2,000 members of Crystal Cathedral are engaged in active volunteer ministry. There are 700 lay ministers of pastoral care who do the basic shepherding of the believers. Twenty-five have been trained as paraprofessional psychological counselors, who can handle all but the most severe personal needs of the church members. The New Hope Counseling Center, a telephone ministry, employs 350 trained volunteers. There are lay ministers of evangelism and of hospitality, and lay ministers who are ushers, greeters, tour guides, and members of the thirty choirs. Specialized ministries have been developed for the poor, the hungry, prisoners, retarded people, convalescents, the handicapped, child-abuse victims, juvenile delinquents, and the emotionally ill. This is not the only church that has succeeded in maintaining strong pastoral leadership while avoiding clericalism. Many growing churches have done it.

The body of Christ differs in its internal design from any human institution. It is an organism with Christ as the head and every member functioning with one or more spiritual gifts — unearned gifts given by God in his grace and wisdom. "God put every part in the body just as he wanted it to be" (1 Cor. 12:18). To the degree that every member of a given congregation has discovered, developed, and is using his or her spiritual gifts, the congregation can be said to be healthy.

And healthy churches grow. The relationship between spiritual gifts and church growth is made clear in one of the major New Testament passages on the gifts: "So when each separate part works as it should, the whole body grows" (Eph. 4:16). Such growth includes, of course, both quality growth and quantity growth.

Part of the leadership function of a church growth pastor is to match people with their God-given ministry roles. This is illustrated by a split-level spectrum (Fig. 2).

Toward the left of this spectrum, the pastor is the minister. This means the pastor is expected to do just about everything that happens in the church except sit in the pews during the worship service — lead people to Christ, counsel believers who have problems, visit the sick in the hospital and at home, monitor the spiritual life of each believer, say grace at church suppers, publish the bulletin and the newsletter, pay the bills, make a pastoral call to each home every year, write letters to visitors, keep in touch with college students and armed service personnel, distribute food to the needy at Christmas time, and preach forty-eight sermons a year. Failure in any of these is likely to draw the comment, "Well, what are we paying the pastor for, anyhow?" The growth potential for a church on this side of the spectrum is very low.

Growth potential increases as the pastor becomes less of a minister and more of a leader. This takes place if the people in the congregation decide to become ministers through the use of their spiritual gifts — teaching, exhortation, service, mercy, evangelism, hospitality, healing, liberality, administration, and others — and the body becomes alive.

The pastor uses his or her gifts also in this ideal situation; but above all, the pastor leads the others. The pastor is more an equipper for ministry than a doer of ministry. (Some use the word "enabler" to mean equipping the saints for ministry.) Rather than being perceived by the congregation as their employee to do their work, the pastor is seen as a recruiter of others to do the tasks of the church. And as the church grows, particularly past that awkward range of 150–250 members, the pastor must be willing to shift from what Lyle Schaller calls a "shepherd" mode to a "rancher" mode. The rancher no longer cares for the sheep one-on-one as the shepherd does. The rancher recruits and trains a number of shepherds to provide the one-on-one care, and then he monitors the whole operation to see that it is properly done.

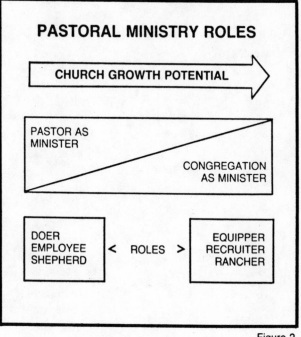

Figure 2

Thus, the pastor's major role for growth is to lead. The congregation's major role is to minister. Although maintaining the proper relationship between the two will not solve every growth problem for every church, it will help unlock tremendous opportunities for growth in many churches now bogged down in unwieldy pastor-congregation relationships.

T W O

CLIMATE CONTROL: CONDITIONS OF A GROWING CHURCH

A cold church, like butter, will not spread. Growing churches have learned how to regulate the congregational thermostat, and they have set it on friendly.

HERB MILLER

No greater love hath anyone than someone who will give up a parking space to visitors.

LYLE SCHALLER

The best-laid fields of farmers can be turned into mud by a week of constant, heavy rain. Every season's crop depends on the climate, which is completely out of their control.

Donald Gerig found that churches, too, are dependent on climate, that "atmospheric conditions" have to be right if a church is going to attract new people and grow. Unlike the weather, however, a church's climate can be shaped favorably by informed leaders.

Now the president of Fort Wayne Bible College, Gerig wrote this chapter out of his experience as pastor of Calvary Memorial Church in Oak Park, Illinois. This church weatherman takes a look at six atmospheric conditions that attract people and thus contribute to growth.

After more than twenty years of pastors' conferences, I had heard my share of formulas for church growth, revival, and renewal. I had done the "pastoral drool" while listening to stories of skyrocketing attendance. I, too, had visited other churches hoping to find the key to growth. But the only church growth I had ever experienced was the plodding, gradual growth that no one writes books about. It seemed a dream for us to consistently have more than five hundred on Sunday morning.

Then it happened! We started seeing our monthly attendance rates 30 percent ahead of the previous year. Before we could get used to that, we found ourselves with more than seven hundred in worship. How did it happen?

The disconcerting thing was that we really couldn't put our finger on any single cause. I couldn't give any glorious stories of personal renewal to account for the growth — God had been good to me throughout my years there. No new programs had been introduced.

Yes, we had moved into a new building, but that was five

years before. And yes, some families had transferred in from a troubled church across town, but the significant growth spurt did not start until later.

It began to dawn on me that what attracted these people, more than anything else, was our "climate." Realizing how intangible that word is, I began to analyze it, and I discovered we had encouraged the components of a growth climate for several years without even realizing it.

In that reverse way, I learned an important lesson. Programs seldom produce the spiritual dynamic necessary for growth; rather, the right spiritual climate produces programs that enhance growth. That's why you can visit seven growing churches and discover seven different programming emphases. In each case, the right climate already existed and became the fuel for effective programming.

What we need, then, is a clearer understanding of the components of a healthy climate. From our experiences and those of other growing churches, I've identified six atmospheric conditions that contribute to growth. These are the elements common to growing churches regardless of their specific programs.

1. A Positive Atmosphere

I risk beginning with an overworked topic, but still it is true: Growing churches emphasize what God *can* do, not what we cannot do; what is best in people, not what is worst; how we can build each other up, not tear each other down.

This has to begin at a personal level. Every church has an ample supply of negative people. What's desperately needed to balance these are other individuals who practice a positive faith in their walk with God as well as in their relationships with people.

Walking through our sanctuary one Sunday morning while the choir was rehearsing, I overheard the director say, "I refuse to have a bad performance today. We will get this right!" The choir laughed, rehearsed one more time, and did a magnificent job in the service that day. That happened partly because one person decided to expect the best. He chose to have positive expectations.

The runaway bestseller *The One-Minute Manager* reminded us to be eager to catch people doing something right rather than always looking for something wrong. That spirit is catching!

When individuals with that attitude relate both to other individuals as well as to God, a climate of expectation can begin to build. The emphasis in a church can begin to shift toward what we can do with God's help. Challenges can be dreamed and accepted.

At one point we had a special drive to raise $100,000 toward the building debt. The willingness to accept that challenge was simply the logical extension of a positive spirit that had grown in the church over several years. Had the climate not been right, the challenge could not have been accepted.

By the way, on the last day of the campaign, receipts passed $103,000.

2. Trust

The burden in creating a climate of trust rests on the one wanting to be trusted, not the one being asked to trust. You don't command trust; you earn it. At the risk of sounding trite, it must be said that trust exists when people are trustworthy.

There is no magic to trustworthiness. For church leaders, it means "going by the book." I'm sure part of the trust I earned came because I never tried to circumvent the established order for operation. That meant presenting proposals to the proper boards or committees before action was begun. It also meant being willing to "lose" graciously on an idea and not seek other means of implementing my plan. It meant living by the budget and not seeking to get what I wanted by "special gifts."

Once I proposed an organizational change at our church that involved revising the constitution. It went through the appropriate study committee and the church board before going to the congregation. At the congregational meeting, it was increasingly apparent that this revision was being resisted. I could have fought. But I chose to lose gracefully on that issue, and to this day they're using the old system and making it work. We made no back-door attempts to circumvent the congregation's wishes. And it paid off with a level of trust among us that made progress possible.

If I were to lock horns with our lay leadership or congregation on an issue I felt could not be compromised, I would either have had to persuade them to my position openly or leave. I would never resort to underhanded means of getting my way. Trust is too important to take that lightly.

3. Excellence

Excellence in ministry is not one arbitrary line that measures all situations. If so, we could paint the perfect church and all seek to imitate it. Instead, excellence is each of us, individually and congregationally, doing our best with the unique resources and limitations we have.

Too often we've made peace with mediocrity, rationalizing our substandard efforts. People are not attracted to that. Our goal must always be our *best* in every part of ministry. This emphasis on excellence is nothing more than being consistent with the glory of God (1 Cor. 10:31). God deserves our best — whether in the way bulletins are printed or how sermons are preached — and that level of excellence is a key ingredient in a climate of growth.

For several years in a row, our church hosted a concert by the Chicago Staff Band of the Salvation Army. This outstanding brass band is built on excellence, fine music, and clear testimony. It was interesting to watch our crowds grow from year to year. We didn't increase our advertising, but people came to know this band would always be at its best.

That can happen to an entire church. If people know we will be at our best in ministry, methods, and facilities, they respond.

4. Oriented to Outreach

Ingrown never equals *growing*. Many churches establish an antigrowth climate without even realizing it by allowing their predominant focus to become the needs of those already in the church. This, I'll admit, is the easiest path to follow, but it will not produce growth.

The mentality of a growing church is continually one of reaching out to others. Even the personal development of current members will be seen in light of increasing their ability to care genuinely about others and minister to them. The minute we start to plan for others rather than ourselves, we create a climate in which we develop and the church will grow.

This, of course, is easier said than done. Every step we take to facilitate ministry to those outside our congregation causes us to struggle past our own comfort. At one point we went to two worship services and two Sunday school sessions to make it possible to handle more people in our present facilities. Though there is nothing unique about this plan, we had to rethink our commitment to outreach. As long as our growth demanded no change from us, it was comfortable. But the minute we had to attend at different hours, divide classes, get used to new teachers, and face the recruitment of additional lay staff, the "cost" of outreach became apparent. Because of their commitment to outreach, however, our people made the changes.

The same outreach mentality spawned new ministries — ministries that attempted to say we care about others, such as support groups for the divorced and for parents of wayward children.

5. Flexibility

The willingness to experiment, to innovate, and even to fail are part of flexibility. You cannot program this spirit, nor can you command it, but a few people placed in key positions can model it. Both by their own flexibility as well as their ability to allow (even encourage) such flexibility in others, the attitude can spread.

Perhaps a strategic time for instilling this spirit is after someone has taken initiative and flubbed.

I felt we started to see this spirit when a holiday outreach activity ended up going poorly. I'm not proud of that failure, but I was pleased we could fail without its becoming an all-consuming issue. Rather, our attitude was one of appreciation for the willingness of those who planned the program — at least they were doing their best to reach out. We learned some things about outreach events, and more importantly, we demonstrated love in spite of failure. That encourages true flexibility.

Another element is the ability to adapt. Almost no program is so good that it never needs to be changed. We have recently tried to identify whether various evangelistic programs are "sowing, cultivating, or reaping" events. That means we must try to understand the people we're trying to reach and plan events to reach them where they are. Ten-year-old programs probably will not work, because people have changed in those ten years.

When the climate is right, when risks are allowed and even traditional events can be adapted, it helps develop sensitivity to the changing culture around us, which is essential to effective ministry and church growth.

6. A Serving Spirit

In a sense, the serving spirit is a summary of a growth climate. Where people truly want to serve and minister, they will be positive, trustworthy, devoted to excellence, oriented to outreach, and flexible.

Just about everything in our society, however, militates against this spirit. It takes a conscious effort to serve rather than be served. We are encouraged today to look out for ourselves or be "fulfilled" (whatever that means). Every opportunity ends up being viewed in light of what we can get out of it.

This attitude easily turns around our relationship to God 180 degrees. Instead of asking what we can do for God, we find ourselves wondering what God can do for us. Christians raised on a pop faith that suggests God is little more than a handy, 24-hour, heavenly banking service find it hard to relate to words like *service* or, worse yet, *sacrifice*.

Thus in church we catch ourselves asking *if* people want to serve. Put that way, of course, many choose not to, and so dies the growth climate. A better way is to start with the assumption that God's people *will* serve. The question is not *if* people will serve, but *where* and *how* they'll serve.

Again, these components of a growth climate cannot be programmed. Rather, they can only be practiced and modeled. They won't begin with action but with attitudes. They will not be limited to certain settings but will be applicable to all situations. Whatever style church growth may take, underneath will be an atmosphere that is positive, trusting and trustworthy, devoted to excellence, oriented to outreach, flexible, and committed to service.

The beauty is that a growth climate doesn't have to wait for action by the official board. One individual can begin to model the components of this climate and have an incredible influence. Obviously, when church leaders are the models, growth can happen more quickly. But any person can be the first line of influence.

I recall sitting in a restaurant one Christmas Day. I went in expecting the atmosphere to be grim. After all, who wants to work on Christmas? Much to my surprise, however, it was almost like walking in on a party. One waitress had obviously decided that if she was going to have to work, she would make the best of it. She had bells tied on her shoes and was joking with customers. She was having a great time, and thanks to her, so was everyone else in the restaurant.

Perhaps that's what it takes in each of our churches — one or two people determined to influence the climate of the church. We may not be able to change weather conditions, but when it comes to the church atmosphere, we can not only survive the elements, but also adjust them to help the harvest.

THREE

MAKING THE SMALL CHURCH VISITOR-FRIENDLY

The most expensive piece of furniture in the church is the empty pew.

ST. JOHN'S NEWSLETTER

A church that is not reaching out is passing out.

DUKE BARRON

If you pastor a small church, you may have read this far and thought, That's great for the big folks, but what about me with my 80 people and $45,000 budget? What can *we* do to appeal to visitors and draw them into our fellowship?

Gary Harrison, pastor of Faith Baptist Church in Delevan, Wisconsin, explains how in the small church as much as in any other, practical steps can be taken to create the right atmosphere. And they don't have to be giant steps, either. Small things can make a big difference. Drawing on over a decade as pastor in a small church, he outlines three principles that helped set and keep his congregation on a steady, upward path of growth.

There I was, settling into my first full-time pastorate and wondering, *What have I gotten myself into?* With a consistent attendance of less than fifteen and a total church budget of under $14,000, you might say there was nowhere to go but up. But how do you begin the ascent?

The people looked to me for leadership, but I wasn't sure I knew where to start, let alone where to lead.

Although my situation was probably extreme, in principle it illustrates what all small-church pastors face at one time or another. With limited resources, a handful of people, and not infrequently a hint of discouragement or desperation, what can a pastor do to make a difference, especially when the budget restrains experimentation? From my more than ten years in a small church, I have learned three principles that helped keep us growing. The principles are not earth-shattering, but they set the stage for growth.

A Positive Perspective

In smaller churches, I have observed what I call the "attitudes vs. abilities" factor. Organizations that work with churches often offer resources to sharpen leaders' skill levels. Such resources, of course, are both good and needed. Rarely, however, do they address the self-image of the church. It is often that deficient attitude, not just the lack of skills, that hinders a church's development.

The small church knows full well what it can't do, how much money it doesn't have, and all the needs it isn't meeting. (Interestingly, it's a revelation to many small-church leaders that bigger churches often feel exactly the same way but on a larger scale.) Such attitudes often lead to an unhealthy introspection and an apologetic demeanor: "Well, I know it's not much, but we're giving it our best shot." The pastor then complicates the situation by directing sermons at the weak areas, urging greater commitment, greater efforts in evangelism, greater giving.

I've found it better to continually hold before my people the good things the church is accomplishing. Even small things, when lumped together, give a sense of real accomplishment to the people.

For example, as I looked at my church early in my tenure, I realized we were not accomplishing much that I thought we needed to do. But rather than constantly emphasize what we couldn't do, I decided to help the people rejoice in the ministry we were able to accomplish.

The local Youth for Christ group was led largely by people in our church; per capita, we were near the top in giving to our district ministries; our participation in conference camping and church-planting programs contributed to our district's outreach; and in many other ways we were making our mark. Individually, none of these accomplishments appeared all that significant, but taken together, they formed a positive backdrop for ministry and for change. When one of our people accomplished something, we made sure our whole church heard about it and rejoiced!

Pastors are often advised to perform a "strengths vs. weaknesses" study of their churches. When the results are tabulated, frequently there is only a weak nod in the direction of the strengths while the major effort is expended on improving the weaknesses. Perhaps a better starting point would be targeting one or two strengths and working to improve them even more, making them the central thrust of the church's ministry.

In most churches, two or three strengths will naturally bubble to the surface. A strength may be fellowship, a good Bible study program, small groups, the worship on Sunday, or an effective children's program. I encourage smaller churches to take charge of the process rather than just letting strengths develop haphazardly. Churches can identify and improve on their strengths until they become expert in these areas.

Developing a strength accomplishes two things. First, it gives the church an area of expertise. Very likely this strength will establish the church's reputation in the community and become a natural springboard for outreach. "You know, there's just something about First Baptist; you really feel loved when you go there, and it makes you want to go back" or "Bible Fellowship definitely understands the problems of young marrieds. I like it there."

Second, it gives the church a reason for genuine and healthy pride. Nothing helps a small church's esteem so much as to know "We do this well!"

When I got to Faith Baptist, I found a group of people who definitely cared about others, member and visitor alike. So I capitalized on it, underscoring at every possible occasion, "We care about people." Lately I've found it rebounding. I had one counselee tell me, "I'm not a churchgoer, but this is a church I'd like to be a part of because you people really care." He'd been to only one service, but he had picked up on a natural strength of our congregation.

Of course, work still remains to round out the total ministry of the church and strengthen its weaknesses. But now it can be done in a positive and progressive atmosphere of growth, not a negative one of desperation and despair. Even in the worst of situations, such strengths become an anchor point for the rest of the ministry.

Pulling is more effective than pushing, and if the people perceive their role as "rounding out" instead of "desperately hanging on," more is accomplished.

A Clear Purpose

Purpose comes second for a definite reason. Often the smaller church has no clear purpose, and the idea of developing a church purpose can strike fear in the hearts of church leaders. Where do we start? How do we proceed? And how can we convince the church it's even necessary?

Sitting down cold and trying to state on paper their reason for being is often just too big a step for church leaders. To be "spiritual," the church will try to do a little bit of everything. A large church may pull it off, but it becomes difficult, if not impossible, with a small church's limited staff and budget.

If, however, the church has already specialized in one or two areas, grasping the concept of purpose and direction is much simpler. The process then becomes one of understanding the scriptural mandates for churches, seeing where the church is going, and developing a purpose that combines the two by saying: (1) "As we understand the Bible, the church is to do . . ." (2) "We can fulfill that mandate by . . ." This way, rather than forcing a purpose on the church, purpose emerges out of the gifts and natural aptitudes of the church.

For example, at Faith Baptist our general purpose statement reflects our desire to keep people, not programs, a central focus of our ministry, and yet to grow at the same time. As we analyzed our ministry, this purpose statement became an indication of both our present direction and our future hopes: "The purpose of our church is to maintain a personal ministry that equips individual believers to successfully live a Christ-like life. We are committed to excellence in (1) preparing the individual, (2) exhibiting a personal touch in ministry, and (3) proclaiming Christ to our world."

I realize that's a pretty broad statement, and we're taught that purposes should be specific. But this was the first time our church had been able to put down in writing our reason for existing. We can now begin to measure all we do against this standard. "Does this activity help us accomplish either number 1, 2, or 3? Are we doing this with excellence? If not, perhaps we should rethink it."

After this first step is taken, further refinement of specific goals comes more easily. For instance, we can take a three-year approach, emphasizing one point each year. Once the original hurdle is overcome, the possibilities are endless.

I admit my entire congregation may not understand completely the purpose and goals of the church — that's the ideal to work toward, but in the interim, I consider it crucial that the leaders do. For a small church like mine to be effective, the leaders must be "owners" of the ministry, not simply administrators. Here I, as pastor, am important: I must encourage, lift, build, help, and show that I value my leaders. They must feel they are colaborers in Christ. And though at this time they may not be able to spell out exactly the goals and direction of the church, they must at least sense a target on the horizon. Remember, the definition of a fanatic is "one who redoubles his efforts when he loses sight of his goal."

All this presupposes that I as pastor have a clear understanding of that target; if I cannot decide what I want the church to become, there will be no dynamic to the church's ministry. I need to be able to say, "In one year, five years, ten years, twenty years I want my church to be . . ." Vision is more caught than taught, and woe unto the pastor who has no vision to spread.

When I arrived at this church, I decided to first dream dreams without worrying about how to make them happen. For the initial year, my goal was simple survival. Within five years I wanted to help the church iron out its problems, stabilize the budget, and move toward an attendance of forty. By ten years I wanted to see a self-supporting congregation on firm footings, one I could leave without its falling apart. After getting the dreams in place, we have worked hard to make them happen, and we are about two years ahead of the plan.

Now I'm beginning to revise the picture. As of this writing, we're looking toward adding a second pastor in a year, buying property and erecting a building in the next three years, and reaching 250 in attendance by five years. Then we'll start a daughter church. This may have seemed impossible when I began with 15 people and practically no resources, but by now it isn't just my vision; others share the dreams with me.

A Thoughtful Presentation

I'm an amateur radio operator, and two stores in my area cater to ham radio needs. One, about fifty miles away, has a prominently displayed sign that reads: THIS IS NOT A RADIO CLUB — NO LOITERING. The other, almost twice the distance, greets you with a pot of coffee and donuts. I drive the extra distance because I feel welcome there.

Similarly, visitors gauge how friendly a church is by the way it presents itself. Smaller churches may unknowingly project a negative image. Buildings are sometimes old, and there's not always money for proper upkeep. Bulletins and church literature may look decidedly amateuristic. The people of the church don't often see these things because the church is so familiar. Perhaps they have never known any other standard. However, these clues do not escape the notice of the first-time visitor. The physical plant and public image communicate the personality of the church.

Beyond the material considerations stand the people themselves: how they react to visitors and how they treat each other. No matter how much the church wants to reach out, growth will not happen if the building and the people fail to say "Welcome!"

One technique I've found helpful in building this awareness is to walk church members through their building as if they were first-time visitors. I take a small group a block or so away from the church, give them pencils and note cards, and try to create a "first-time visitor" mindset for them. Then we "visit" our church. What does the general appearance of the building and grounds communicate about the congregation? How at home do they feel? For example, can they find the rest rooms without having to ask the embarrassing question? Is the foyer cluttered and messy? Are minor repairs left undone? Do the walls and posters tell them anything? If one is not a Christian and has seldom been to church, what would this building say? Would they have any idea where to go or what they were supposed to do? The unwritten "signs" around the building may say a lot more than any welcoming committee ever does.

When the group "visited" our building, they found the exterior in sad shape. It looked as if we were telling the community we weren't a viable church; if the building were any indication, we might not be around much longer. However, on the interior we scored better. Our friendly bulletin boards and displays and the inviting coffee pot in the foyer made up for the undumped trash and the woeful lack of signs indicating rest rooms.

Since then we've spruced up our exterior, made sure the trash is dumped regularly, and posted clear signs to the lavatories. These simple efforts may not win any souls, but they tell people we are committed to our church and care about them. And that, combined with our strength of friendliness, may bring them back to hear the gospel.

I apply the same technique to the Sunday activities. Is any effort made to create a good impression? Or is too much taken for granted? How many people talk to visitors? How much time elapses before someone greets newcomers? Does the church give any impression that it even expects someone new to come? For one new church I know, meeting in a community center, it took twenty minutes of deliberate search inside the building for a visitor to find the meeting location! The church had no signs posted, no ushers at the outside doors — and no visitors.

I try to extend image-oriented thinking to all the public images our church projects. What does the Sunday bulletin look like? Although it did cost our church a bit of money (at a time when we had little to spare), we custom designed our bulletins. Since bulletins generally go home with people, we wanted them to carry away a good impression, so we bore the expense. We've had T-shirts professionally designed with our church logo. We use them for sports, youth activities, vacation Bible school, and other occasions, and it's exciting to see them dot the town.

I've found that whatever we decide to do — even as a small church — we need to maintain a sharp image before the community, one that says, "We know what we're doing, and we intend to do it well." People are, after all, bombarded by TV and print media of the highest quality, and it hits a responsive chord if the church is professional in its presentation. Would people feel comfortable visiting a doctor whose office is kept with the carelessness with which many churches keep their foyers?

This, of course, is not to negate the church's spiritual ministry role. But with a little attention to detail and, yes, just a little money, much "pre-evangelism" can be accomplished with first-time visitors before any words are spoken or any visits made. And the members themselves begin to take pride in their church as well.

The determination of salmon swimming upstream to spawn impresses me. I feel tired just watching them. However, there is no spiritual blessing to be received by churches fighting their way upstream against feelings of insignificance and defeat. Effective ministry is difficult enough even in the best of situations.

I've discovered these three principles are neither costly nor difficult to implement, yet they can help churches overcome self-image deficits.

My father used to tell me, "Work smart, not just hard." I believe our Father honors the same concept. By taking a good look at our churches and making sure some basic principles are at work, we can set the stage for growth and service in the smaller church that could make even big churches envious.

F O U R

FRESH AIR FOR EVANGELISM TRAINING

The way from God to a human heart is through a human heart.

Samuel Gordon

The world is far more ready to receive the Gospel than Christians are to hand it out.

George W. Peters

"I know I'm supposed to witness, but I tried it once, and I felt like a door-to-door vacuum cleaner salesman, trying to sell something nobody really wanted. After that I told myself, Never again." Most pastors have heard something like that over and over.

Getting people to do personal evangelism is one of the toughest challenges we face. Many parishioners remain plagued by fear, guilt, and negative attitudes in this area, and consequently they don't reach out to others. How can we get around these walls of inactivity to make effective witnesses out of ordinary Christian lay people?

Becky Pippert, an evangelism specialist with Inter-Varsity Christian Fellowship, has found keys to making personal witness both enjoyable and fruitful. From years of experience in the field, she shows how one-on-one evangelism can be changed from an "ought to" to a "want to."

I've discovered that most church folk, whatever their denomination, have a similar reaction to evangelism: "That's just not my cup of tea, thank you." You can almost hear the iron gates clanging shut in their minds.

When I ask people why they don't evangelize, I've heard:

"I've never been fond of imposing something on someone."

Or, as one Reed College student so succinctly put it, *"Evangelism* is how many people I've offended this week."

Or one of my favorites, "You know, I *would* evangelize if I didn't love people so much."

Most Christians are so afraid of being labeled part of the lunatic fringe that they say nothing about their faith, save in the friendly confines of the church. Any effective evangelism training begins by realizing people are plagued by guilt, fear, and negative attitudes, which must be identified and exorcised before we can get anywhere.

Where do these negative attitudes come from? No Christian group has as its conscious aim "Let's totally violate their personhood and mow them over for Jesus." Yet that's the stereotype: buttonholing and forcing tracts on people.

I've been amazed how consistent church people are in their reasons for *not* evangelizing. And the reasons are nearly always what evangelism should never be in the first place.

Most Christians intuitively know that evangelism belongs not in the sales department but in the context of loving relationships. Common sense tells us we must both proclaim the Word and live it out among the people our lives naturally intersect. Whenever evangelism majors in technique and strategy and minors in love and respect for individuals, we've gotten into trouble.

But some of us have swung too far the other way, majoring in relationships and minoring in a clear proclamation of the gospel and the call to commitment. The result is mere friendship and no evangelism.

How do we avoid the extremes and encourage a biblical evangelism that is sensitive and loving, respectful of the individual? I'd like to suggest three elements that need to be part of our training.

The first two have been suggested by Gabriel Fackre, who says we must get the story straight and get the story out. I'd like to add that we must take the story in, meaning that our training must deepen our spiritual resources as well as build content and communication skills.

Getting the Story Straight

We in the West always have been fairly effective in stating gospel truth through theological propositions or four-point outlines. We are now beginning to discover what our brothers and sisters in the East have known all along — truth is also communicated through storytelling.

I recently read how Lewis Alemen breaks down the verbal message into three parts: (1) telling God's story — the drama of his deeds, particularly the life, death, and resurrection of Christ; (2) telling my story — which isn't the gospel message but illustrates its power; and (3) telling their story — how God's story relates to the person to whom we are witnessing.

Genuine witnessing integrates all three stories. I've found, however, that most people need special help in learning how to tell the Lord's story. We usually can explain the gospel through outlines and diagrams. But can we talk about Jesus in a way that makes him come alive? Can we tell his story and parables in a way that others can see their relevance for daily life?

One of my frequent activities as an Inter-Varsity staff member was giving evangelistic "dorm talks" in which I would speak to skeptical students about Christianity (usually dealing with apologetics) and then would open it up for questions. The atmosphere frequently was stimulating and charged. Often we would have a lively debate into the wee hours.

Then one day I heard a colleague and popular speaker, Gene Thomas, give a "dorm talk" at a college in Washington state. To my surprise, he simply described what Jesus was like as a person and the things Jesus valued — people, in particular. He spoke of the quality of relationships Jesus desired and indeed enabled us to have. As he spoke, my first thought was, *But they need to know it's true and logical.* My second thought: *If you're going to talk about Jesus, shouldn't you discuss the cross?*

When it came time for questions, the students spoke on a very personal level: how competitive and insecure they felt, how much they abhorred phoniness and elitism. They voiced their surprise that Jesus was concerned with such things. There also were valid questions about the truth of Jesus' claims, but the atmosphere was one of beauty and grace.

As we filed out, three seniors went to Gene and said, "In all our years here, being on various committees and going to meetings, we've never experienced a meeting like this, where people were so open and there was so much love and acceptance."

Gene casually said, "Oh, well, that's because Jesus is here. We feel these qualities because that's exactly what Jesus is like."

They looked at Gene with wide-eyed astonishment, and I realized then that more had been accomplished evangelistically than in any of my dorm talks. They hadn't been converted, they still didn't understand the whole gospel, they still had lots of unanswered questions, but they had been tremendously attracted to Jesus. It was a vital beginning. Later when we asked if anyone would like to study the person of Jesus in the Gospels, an unusual number signed up. That experience confirmed what I had been growing to suspect: I needed to rediscover Jesus and be able to communicate him in fresh and descriptive ways to make my evangelism more effective.

A few months later, I arrived at Harvard during a one-month speaking tour. Instead of the rather cerebral talk I had planned, I decided to follow Gene's example and speak about Jesus. I retold one of Jesus' own stories, in this case the parable of the Prodigal.

The body language of the group was fascinating. I walked into a room jammed with bright, skeptical students, some looking hostile, some looking as if it were great sport. Many were slunk back in their chairs, looking amused and waiting for a chance to attack. As I began telling the parable, I noticed the change. They couldn't help getting involved in the story. Slouches turned to straight backs, and finally to bodies leaning forward in their chairs. Then I drew theological principles and opened it for questions. While the questions weren't especially different from those asked in other dorm discussions, the students' attitude had changed dramatically — from hostility and arrogance to genuine interest, curiosity, and involvement.

What this taught me, first, was the power of a good story. Everybody loves a story, partly because it utilizes both sides of the brain, sparking our creative, imaginative side as well as the conceptual, rational part of us. And the Gospels are full of wonderful stories, packed with profound theological truth about God and ourselves. To a nonbeliever who does not have a theological framework, an isolated Bible verse may not make sense. But if we tell a story out of life — as Jesus' stories were — and since life is already a shared framework, the meaning of the story may take root.

Again, I'm not suggesting we abandon our gospel outlines or theological propositions or apologetics. I'm merely saying let's *add* to our evangelistic repertoire the ability to talk about Jesus in natural and fresh ways and to tell his stories spontaneously and freely.

Getting the Story Out

Jesus always seemed to be doing two things: asking questions and telling stories. Christians always seem to be doing two other things: giving answers and "preaching."

All four are necessary — at the right time and in the right place. But we tend to forget that the God of the Bible was an extraordinary communicator; we ignore Jesus' example of how to start a conversation, and we jump in prematurely with answers and sermonettes before the listener's curiosity is aroused.

I frequently ask people at a conference to tell me where they struggle in witnessing. Their answers fall into three categories: 2 percent say they struggle with intellectual questions they can't answer; 1 percent say they struggle with mechanics (How do I lead a person to Christ?); and 97 percent say they need help with their communication skills (How do I move from secular conversation to spiritual in a natural way? How do I disagree or not participate in an activity without seeming "holier than thou"? How can I be myself when I feel the world puts me in a Christian box?).

It seems ironic that so much current evangelism training focuses so heavily on content skills when people seem to be saying they need more help with communication skills. Again, it's not an issue of either/or, but both/and. We certainly need to know what to say, but we also need to know *how* to say it.

The communication process is so complex and multifaceted that it's easy to feel overwhelmed. The key to all good communication is the ability to love as Christ loved. Jesus constantly taught that if we're to be his followers, our lives must bear the stamp of profound love — to God and to our neighbor. Our lives must be dominated by his love, not merely religious activity. How we treat people will be the clearest signal to them of what God is like. Nobody wants to be someone's evangelistic project. People want to be loved and taken seriously.

I've seen Christians who've broken nearly every rule of communication and yet have been effective evangelists because they genuinely loved the person they were talking to. Ultimately, love is everything.

After establishing Christ's love as the foundation for communication, we can analyze our own communication style, finding our strengths and weaknesses: Are we shy and timid? Is it difficult for us to start a conversation, much less get it around to God? Do we miss detecting people's needs? Do we listen well?

There is surprisingly little in the Christian market in this area. Certainly, James Engel's *Contemporary Christian Communications: Its Theory and Practice* and Em Griffin's *The Mind Changers* are good resources. The secular research on information and communication theory is also beneficial.

I've found it immensely helpful to devise relational exercises for the specific communication skills I'm trying to teach: listening skills, affirming skills, dealing with hostility, disagreeing without being disagreeable, and so on.

For instance, information theorists tell us that to communicate effectively, we must recognize our own stereotypes of the person to whom we're speaking. So I developed this exercise: I say, "Turn to the person next to you. Assume this is a Christian friend. I want one of you to say, 'Hi. How was your weekend?' Then the other person needs to reply where he or she has been this weekend and one thing he or she learned from the conference."

After a few minutes, I then say, "Now reverse the roles. This time the other person says, 'How was your weekend?' and you answer. But this time you know the person asking the question is not a Christian."

The contrast in reactions from step one and step two couldn't be more stark. In step one, everyone chatters, and the atmosphere is relaxed. After step two, there is initial silence, then groans, nervous laughter, and uneasiness. Afterward I ask them to tell me how they felt in going from one to the next. The answer is always the same: "I felt fine and relaxed in the first but very uncomfortable in the second. I just knew they wouldn't be interested. I knew they would think I was a jerk. I felt very defensive and uneasy."

Then we examine why, having been told nothing about the person except that he or she wasn't a believer, they assumed the worst. Was that fair? Why did they do it? How did their assumptions affect their ability to communicate? If that's their basic attitude toward every nonbeliever they meet, it's no wonder they feel uncomfortable witnessing.

Then we work on developing different mental attitudes to stop judging others unfairly before we really know them. The helpfulness of these exercises is that it involves people in the learning process. Their minds may have grasped the concept, but it simply takes practice to get our behavior in accord with our minds.

Taking the Story In

Finally, we must be increasingly transformed by the message itself. We don't simply give the gospel — we *are* the gospel.

When Wesley was asked, "Why do people seem to be so drawn to you, almost like a magnet?" he answered, "Well, you see, when you set yourself on fire, people just love to come and see you burn."

That is evangelism: not a program but a fire within.

People will be drawn to the warmth of God's fire within us even though they may not at first be able to name its source. We must continually stoke and feed the fire as we are transformed by the presence of Christ within us through prayer, Bible reading, deeper sensitivities to the Holy Spirit, and learning to walk in the Spirit and not the flesh. All are a part of the resources that make our witnessing powerful and penetrating.

EVANGELISM IN A SMALL TOWN

Witnessing involves all that we are and therefore do; it goes far beyond what we say at certain inspired moments. So the question is not will *we witness, but* how *will we witness?*

PAUL LITTLE

Let's face it: small-town evangelism is especially tough. Most of the people in small towns are well established as either saints or sinners. And trying to change individuals even in the second category may be seen as a disruption of the comfortable status quo.

As Kenneth Vetters, pastor of East Columbus United Methodist Church in Columbus, Indiana, knows from firsthand experience, there are indeed difficult obstacles. But as you read this chapter, you can learn from someone who's already been there, who identifies the hazards and points the way around them.

Small-town evangelism sounds like an oxymoron, a contradiction in terms. With no municipal arenas to rent for crusades and precious few new residents to call on, how does a church pursue evangelism? Don't "revivals" attract only the solidly saved? A few wayward teenagers might be threatened into attending one or two nights, but they usually slip out at half time to smoke in the parking lot.

Most people in the five small Midwestern towns where I've pastored have appeared to be either clean-living church members or well-certified nonbelievers. The lines are clearly drawn and memorized, raising a valid question: *What does evangelism mean in a place with fewer than three stoplights?*

The Needy Are with Us Always

The starting point is to remember that every community has people with needs; some just hide theirs better than others. No village or rural area is without the following three types:

1. Active church members who are not in a right relationship with God. Unless these are evangelized, outreach efforts in a small town will fail, since Christians' lives are always being scrutinized.

2. *Nominal church members.* The children of devout parents, the spouse of the church pillar, the friend from work who occasionally attends church events. . .all these and others have a commitment to the church that is cultural rather than personal.

3. *The unchurched.* Even in the one-gas-station town, where church membership appears all sewn up, some people hide in the crevices. Maybe they moved into the area years ago but kept their membership in a church a hundred miles away. Maybe they quietly dropped out of church over some problem. They may not be hostile to Christianity, but they've never known the difference a joyful, consistent Christian life can make.

I've broadened my definition of evangelism to include reaching very nice, conservative people in small towns; they need to make the same life-changing decision as the most colorful jet setter or drug addict. I've also tried to emphasize not only dramatic, first-time conversions, but also a call to renewal for people at whatever stage of the Christian journey. The result is typically as many people seeking forgiveness and restoration as making first-time decisions to follow Christ.

Overcoming the Obstacles

Small towns have their own psyche. People are very concerned about what their neighbors think, since they know them by first name and may even be shirt-tail relatives. The idea of radical change is suspicious from the start — and that obviously includes the life-altering change of spiritual repentance.

Thus, a number of problems make evangelism challenging:

• *People seem to be pigeonholed.* A young person doesn't move forward at a certain point of Christian growth and is sidelined ever after. People are frozen out when the church doesn't care about them as much as it does about others. Someone more popular or more outgoing gets asked to sing or teach or organize.

My wife remembers one practice session for the annual Christmas cantata when the pianist, a high school girl, was absent. Only then did someone remember that another high school girl in the alto section could also play the piano. She sat down and played the difficult music perfectly. Why had she never been asked before for any kind of program? No one could answer.

This kind of unintended neglect can discourage a church member to the point of dropping out, and no small amount of fervent preaching or witnessing will win them back. Small-town congregations have to pay conscious attention to the gifts and potential of all their members.

• *New people are not always welcome.* One church member, a teacher, frequently complained to me privately that we didn't really need altar calls in the church. He felt they were nothing but emotionalism. Yet he was a staunch supporter of the church and always the first to praise its loving spirit. He couldn't see the connection between the two.

People are attracted to a church's love and care but often don't understand how it got that way. Though they may have come to the church through a series of special meetings, they subsequently question whether the church ought to sponsor such events.

Another area for this tension is the sharing of power. Older members may be eager to place new people as Sunday school teachers or youth leaders but balk at including them on the board of trustees or the finance committee. I frequently remind our nominating committee that *everyone* needs a position of responsibility. Most leadership positions are on a rotating basis in our church, and I think that has something to do with our growth, even though we're in a rural area. If new members are not absorbed into the life of the church, the fruits of our evangelism program will quickly shrink.

I remember in a former congregation how a young family became deeply interested in the Christian life. The wife especially got involved in working with children through a week-day club. Mostly unchurched youngsters came for music, crafts, Bible stories, games, and refreshments. This dedicated woman and her helpers were having an effective outreach.

Were the lay leaders overjoyed? Hardly. They complained about "the little street urchins" messing up the bathrooms and wondered if church property was being stolen. Because of the negative attitude, the new family was driven away to another church, which welcomed their dedication and talents.

• *Social class counts.* Years ago, one of my congregations had just finished a quarterly study on poverty in America and the church's need to reach out with physical and spiritual aid. The course was now ending with the traditional pitch-in meal and program.

Just as the serving began, there was a knock at the church's back door. A ragged-looking family stood beside a beat-up station wagon. The father wanted to know if the church had a fund to help transients; the children were hungry.

Many were distraught that this unkempt family would interrupt a church meeting. Others, fortunately, invited them inside and heaped their plates high with food from the ample potluck table. They also invited the family to stay for the program afterward.

I could hardly contain my smile as I opened the program by telling the group that they had already been given a test on the past three months' study material. I then asked the guests to introduce themselves — a church family from a nearby town who had agreed to play the part of tramps for the evening. It was a memorable moment.

As a small-town pastor, I must continually encourage church members to stretch, to accept all people, even if from a different socioeconomic class or from a family not highly regarded in the community.

• *In generally conservative areas, evangelism often sounds like fanaticism.* In one church, a teenage daughter of long-time church members made a solid decision for Christ. She began studying her Bible and attending the youth meetings. Her parents became upset. Concerned that she had gone off the deep end, they forbade her to attend all but Sunday morning worship.

She became the only girl in town who had to sneak out of the house for a prayer meeting.

Fear of radical Christian living expresses itself as resistance to any kind of emotional response. Perhaps people have been burned by high-pressure tactics in the past or have seen too many shallow conversions fade. Whatever the reason, we must hold to the goal while maintaining a patient, caring attitude. Confrontation and argument don't help. Only Christ's love can free these people from their fears.

• *Lack of Christian maturity always hurts.* The tiny, rural church I served as a student pastor had three gentlemen who would argue over who was the worst sinner. One fellow grew tobacco but didn't smoke it. Another didn't grow it or smoke it but sold it in his store. The third neither grew it nor sold it but did smoke it.

They were joking, but the level of debate says something. In small towns, where everyone knows exactly how everyone else lives, many become enslaved to legalism. They find it easier to follow the prevailing moral codes than to think for themselves how God would have them live. The checklist of do's and don'ts pre-empts opening up to God's leading.

One antidote to this, I have found, is to involve people in witnessing. And in a small town, it doesn't have to be flamboyant. Subtlety goes a long way.

For example, one young father decided to quit playing cards during his lunch break at the local factory and read his Bible instead. The other men, who had known him for years, ridiculed him at first but were intrigued by his discipline. Some were eventually drawn to his church through his unassuming, natural style. Needless to say, his own Christian faith was deepened as he shared his new life with his friends.

Special Meetings:
A Modest Defense

A lot of negative things have been written and said about "revivals," crusades, missions. But in small towns and rural areas, an evangelistic series of meetings can work well. They are still an accepted way for people to be challenged to receive Christ. They are part of a tradition, and tradition is very important in a small community.

In my ministry, special meetings have been a significant element of evangelism. They take work, of course. You can't just set a date and hope people show up. A lot of planning, prayer, and effort by many church members is required.

Several weeks ahead, I usually preach sermons that create anticipation and heighten a feeling of need. My subjects have included how Jesus can make a difference in daily life, and what salvation is and how it's obtained. As the people start to desire spiritual awakening, they become open to the impending meeting.

The precise format varies from denomination to denomination, I know. Preaching, music, and morning study sessions each play a part. But the results can be appreciated by all:

• The services allow people to lay down their burdens (jealousy, hatred, selfishness, a drug dependency, whatever) at a specific time and place, which helps them remember their decision.

• They give people a chance to reconcile long-standing problems with one another.

• They can unite the family generations at the altar.

• They serve as a focus for the entire church.

New Life in the Byways

It takes a lot of courage for a person in a small community to decide for Christ with all his or her friends, relatives, neighbors, and coworkers watching intently. Yet the joyful, consistent Christian life that results can touch many, creating ripples in the placidness of rural living.

Evangelism in a small town may never generate the impressive numbers of big-city crusades and programs, but it is both possible and necessary.

It is also downright thrilling as people's lives are transformed by God's love.

SIX

HOME VISITATION: IT CAN BE EFFECTIVE

No other single factor makes a greater difference in improving annual membership additions than an immediate visit to the homes of first-time worshipers.

HERB MILLER

Visitation: the image that immediately comes to mind is of knocking on a stranger's door as the glow from a television leaks through the front drapes. What's this person going to think of me? *you're likely to worry in such a situation.* Am I going to interrupt a favorite program? Will they want to talk, or will they resent my visit? *And perhaps most troubling of all,* Is it really going to make any difference?

To find out, LEADERSHIP *surveyed nearly seven hundred people who had been contacted in the course of a year by the calling programs of three diverse churches. Marshall Shelley, managing editor of* LEADERSHIP, *studied the results and reports on what people think about being visited in their homes. Besides describing how people respond, he explains what approaches led to the best results.*

What do they really think —
those people we call on? Do they associate church visitation
teams with the assorted cultists who go door knocking and
pamphlet peddling? How many people are glad to see us, and
how many feel we're invading their privacy?

They're normally civil, perhaps even polite — but pastor
and lay volunteers wonder, *What do they say after we've left?*
And more important, *What effect, if any, did this visit have?*

To find out, LEADERSHIP surveyed nearly seven hundred
people who had been contacted in the past year by the calling
programs of three diverse congregations: Galilee Baptist
Church in Denver, Colorado; Bismark Reformed Church in
Bismarck, North Dakota; and Big Valley Grace Community
Church in Modesto, California.

Each of these churches has weekly visitation based on the
Evangelism Explosion method. The program, which trains
lay people to give a brief, systematic presentation of the gospel, is used by many churches, including these three, to follow up on first-time visitors to their worship services.

These were *not* "cold contacts" — homes picked out of the
phone book or off a city map. These were people who had

shown some interest in the church, usually by attending a Sunday morning service and signing a visitor form.

In order to get candid reactions and the greatest number of responses, the surveys were short — five questions — and anonymous, though people were given the option of including name and phone number if they were willing to talk further. Thirty percent included their names.

In order to assess the effect over time, separate surveys were sent to those visited from September 1982 through August 1983 and those contacted since September 1983.

Because of the strong response (from one group an amazing 74 percent of the surveys were answered) and the similar results from all three churches (despite their different sizes and locations), the survey may indicate what other churches with similar programs can expect.

Generally a Positive Contact

Nearly 80 percent felt good about the visit, and over 60 percent indicated it was either helpful or very helpful.

In response to the question "After they left, what were your personal feelings about the visit?" less than 1 percent marked *Strongly Negative (They shouldn't have come).* Five percent said *Negative (It was an irritation),* 13 percent were neutral, 44 percent said *Positive (I appreciated their stopping),* and another 35 percent felt *Strongly Positive (I was very glad they came.)* Three percent marked *Other.* (See chart 1.)

Several surveys said, "I was nervous and hesitant at first, but afterward I was glad they'd come." Others were grateful for "meeting people who cared."

Those who were negative complained primarily about the timing of the visit.

"We had just moved to town and were *very* busy laying carpet and cutting the pads underneath in anticipation of the moving van arriving the next morning," wrote one respondent. "When the team called, I explained our predicament

CHART 1

FEELINGS ABOUT THE VISIT

After they left, what were your personal feelings about the visit?

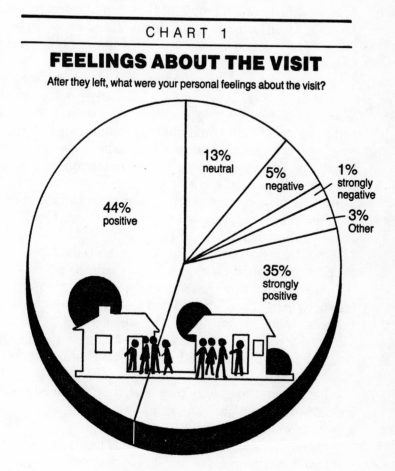

13%
neutral

5%
negative

1%
strongly
negative

3%
Other

44%
positive

35%
strongly
positive

and suggested we meet another time, but they said they only visited that night each week and insisted they come in for a short visit. I felt very uncomfortable — we had no furniture, no refreshments, and were in work clothes. We explained we were Christians already, yet we had to listen to the whole speech because one member of the team 'needed practice.' The 'short' visit lasted an hour and a half, and we were resentful since we had to work into the early morning hours to prepare for the movers."

Several mentioned that the visits came just as they were leaving the house, at bedtime for kids, when someone was sick, or at mealtime. "My husband and I were both in our bathrobes and felt uncomfortable with the unexpected visitors," said one. Another wrote, "My husband had the flu, the house was a disaster, and they came unannounced. I would have appreciated some warning."

Several others commented on the approach of the callers:

"They treated me like a new Christian instead of the person I am — a Christian of twenty-five years."

"Once they discovered I was a Christian, they 'practiced' the plan of salvation on me. I felt like a guinea pig."

These, however, represent a minority. In response to the question "After they left, did you feel you had gained anything by their coming?" only between 3 and 19 percent (depending on the church) said *No, the visit wasn't helpful.* The overwhelming majority said the visit was either somewhat helpful, helpful, or very helpful.

What, if anything, did they feel they'd gained? Most checked more than one response:

Information about the church (69 percent)
Beginning a friendship with the visitor (32 percent)
A further step in my Christian walk (26 percent)
A new understanding about the Christian faith (9 percent)
A new relationship with Jesus Christ (6 percent)
Other (12 percent)

Among those marking *Other*, a few were negative. ("We appreciated the first visit, but after we told them we were active in our own church, they should not have come back *four* more times. It was an irritation.") Most, however, expressed appreciation. "I was glad to see Christians evangelizing rather than the cults," said one man.

Or as a Bismarck woman wrote, "I became a Christian three years before, but I backslid. After this visit I felt as though someone cared. When they left, I rededicated my life to Christ. Now, I've joined a women's Bible study at the church."

Long-term Effects

Survey responses also revealed the church attendance patterns following the visitation.

Overall, 28 percent said they're now regularly attending the church that called on them. Another 12 percent have been back once or twice.

Some 13 percent have visited another church and become active there, and 10 percent were already attending another church and have become more active there.

No change in church involvement was reported by 23 percent, and 14 percent marked *Other*. (See chart 2.)

Another way of looking at it: Based on this sampling, 40 percent of those you visit will wind up back at your church at least once, and a full 50 percent will become more frequent church attenders, either at your church or another.

Often this takes time. While 30 percent of those visited recently claimed no change in church involvement, that number dropped to 18 percent among those visited several months ago. In other words, results sometimes come late; people begin showing up months after the doorbell was first rung.

Where do these unhurried people eventually plug in?

CHART 2

OVERALL CHURCH INVOLVEMENT

Since the visit, has there been any change in your church involvement?

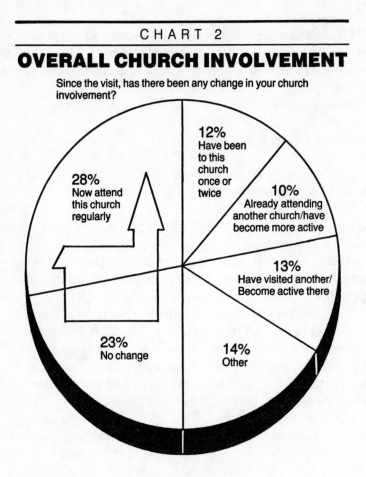

28%
Now attend this church regularly

12%
Have been to this church once or twice

10%
Already attending another church/have become more active

13%
Have visited another/ Become active there

23%
No change

14%
Other

Primarily other churches. (See chart 3.) Of those called on recently, 30 percent are regularly attending that church. For those called on a year ago, the figure dips slightly to 27 percent. But during that year, those becoming more active in *other* churches rises from a combined 14 percent to 29 percent.

If visitation is seen as a ministry for the kingdom of God rather than simply for the specific congregation, this can be encouraging: over half the people you visit will likely become more active at one church or another.

The Fraction We Focus On

Evangelism programs often rate their success by how many people "pray the prayer" committing themselves to Jesus. What about this 6 percent? Who are these people?

Mostly young adults. By age, the new believers fell into these categories:

0–19 years — none
20–35 years — 80 percent
36–50 years — 7 percent
51–65 years — 13 percent
65 years or more — none

Possibly this can be explained because the early adult years are transition years, and those in flux are more receptive to the gospel. It also may be the result of this group's doing more church shopping and thus being the focus of more visitation. (See chart 4.)

In addition, 80 percent of those claiming a new relationship with Jesus Christ marked the response *Took a further step in my Christian walk*. Perhaps this wasn't the first time they had heard the gospel; perhaps they had been getting closer to taking this step for some time.

What part did the visit itself play in their decision? What had been especially influential? We phoned all those who said they'd begun a new relationship with Christ and who'd included their name and phone number.

Slightly over half described the experience as primarily a

CHART 3

CHANGE IN CHURCH ATTENDANCE

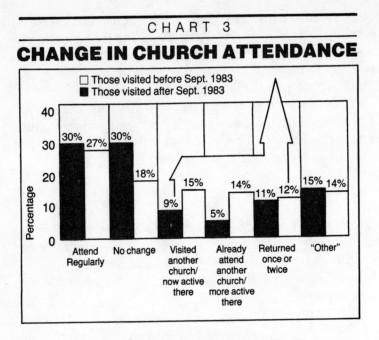

☐ Those visited before Sept. 1983
■ Those visited after Sept. 1983

Percentage

| Attend Regularly | No change | Visited another church/ now active there | Already attend another church/ more active there | Returned once or twice | "Other" |

- Attend Regularly: 30%, 27%
- No change: 30%, 18%
- Visited another church/now active there: 9%, 15%
- Already attend another church/more active there: 5%, 14%
- Returned once or twice: 11%, 12%
- "Other": 15%, 14%

CHART 4

THE AGE FACTOR

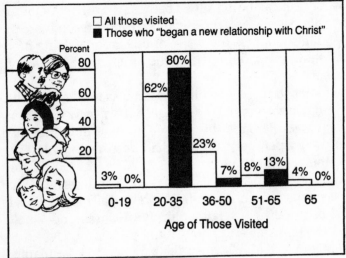

☐ All those visited
■ Those who "began a new relationship with Christ"

Percent

- 0-19: 3%, 0%
- 20-35: 62%, 80%
- 36-50: 23%, 7%
- 51-65: 8%, 13%
- 65: 4%, 0%

Age of Those Visited

renewal of previous religious commitment. "We wanted to get back into following Christ," said the wife of an Air Force officer. "We were puzzled about things in the Bible. They answered our questions and gave us the words to describe our faith."

"I was already a Christian, but I'd sort of gotten away from it," said a young woman in California. "But they were so warm but not pushy; they didn't make me feel like an outcast. They opened my eyes about how people really are — that it's normal to slack off, but you have to keep coming back."

In every case, however, even among those making a first-time commitment, there had been exposure to the gospel before they met with the visitation team.

"I'd been reading the Bible with a Christian girl at work, and I was beginning to understand what God wants," said a Denver woman. "But I had never really prayed to ask Jesus into my life. The people from the church asked if I wanted to, and I said yes. It was my first time 'officially,' and I was real nervous because I didn't know the people. If that had been my first contact with Jesus, I wouldn't have done it."

Another new believer, a medical student, explained, "I grew up (and still am) an Episcopalian, but I never had what I'd call a personal relationship with God. Then I experienced several deaths of people about my age, and I realized that if I was going to be a doctor, I'd better come to terms with death.

"When the group from Galilee came, they explained their faith, and it made sense. They were very supportive but didn't push. They didn't say anything I hadn't heard before, but we prayed together, and it was a big symbolic event, an outward declaration of my faith. It was the beginning of the process of change in my life."

Lessons Learned

After sifting survey returns and interviewing by phone, what can we conclude? What would be helpful for visitation teams to know? Three things stand out:

1. *Calling on people is not offensive.* The strongest finding of this survey is that while some people may be hesitant at first, 80 percent wind up enjoying the attention they receive.

Those who knock on doors without phoning ahead of time have a greater risk of negative response, but as Mike Pentel, a visitation team leader at Galilee Baptist, says, "It's a tradeoff. When you call ahead of time and ask if you can come over, it's easier for them to say no. The people who need it most wouldn't get touched. If we don't find anyone at home several nights in a row, then we'll try to call and set up an appointment."

And unless the time was inconvenient, even those who weren't called appreciated the visit.

Many of those ready to make spiritual decisions, however, are eager to talk and simply waiting for the opportunity. Most of those who'd begun a new relationship with Christ also said they knew the visitors were coming — either someone phoned or someone had talked to them at church. Instead of discouraging anyone from coming over, these people said they were prepared to discuss spiritual things with the visitation team.

2. *Make sure the communication is two-way.* No one surveyed objected to what the callers said. People who've visited a church are interested in what the church stands for. The resistance comes when the message is dispensed as a monologue or sales pitch, with only token responses asked of the listener.

"All the visitor did was tell me the basics of Christianity without ever asking about where I was in my spiritual life," wrote one man. "He rambled on and sought no interaction from me."

Another said, "I didn't get any information about the church — only their personal experiences."

One woman reported, "It was uncomfortable because I was a Christian, but my husband is not. He stood up through the whole visit, hoping they'd leave, though he's too polite to ask them. But one man talked for twenty minutes without stopping. They needed to ask us some questions. It was unnatural."

Interestingly, a year later, that woman was involved herself in the church's visitation program, and she learned from her pastor how to talk about the gospel naturally. "It's much more relaxed that way," she says.

3. *Don't be discouraged if the night doesn't produce a dramatic conversion.* Lay people sometimes get the impression that the evening is less than successful if no one prays to accept Christ. Actually, a profession of faith is the exception, not the rule — one in approximately twenty visits. But that doesn't mean failure. Significant spiritual things are happening.

One woman, for instance, who indicated she'd received help with a personal question or problem, said, "About a month before the people from the church came, my ex-husband kidnapped my son. He came over for a visit, put our son in the car, and left. I haven't seen either of them since.

"I was feeling so guilty — I should have known . . . I should have done something to stop it.

"You never get over those feelings, but the people who visited me from the church really helped. They didn't second-guess me, and they helped me see I didn't need to keep blaming myself. They cared about me.

"I told them I was thinking of taking in an older person to room with me, and within the next week, each of them phoned me with names of people to contact. They kept me going through a rough time."

No, this woman didn't make a profession of faith that night. Nor has she been added to the church rolls — she's only been back once or twice. But that anonymous visitation team showed that ministry, even when it's not visible, can be effective.

SEVEN

THE EVANGELISTIC BIBLE STUDY: MAKING IT WORK

Now the Bereans were of more noble character than the Thessalonians, for they received the message with greater eagerness and examined the Scriptures every day to see if what Paul said was true.

ACTS 17:11

The skeptic who believes the Bible's human authors manufactured their God out of psychological need has not read the Scriptures carefully.

CHARLES COLSON

It works in offices, on college campuses, and in local churches. What is it? The evangelistic Bible study. Can you really get non-Christians involved in such a study? It happens all the time, it changes lives, and it's easier than you may think.

How do you invite people so they say yes instead of slamming doors? Should you study a topic or a book of the Bible? And how do you guide such a study for maximum impact on lives? In this chapter, Marilyn Kunz, one of the leaders of Neighborhood Bible Studies, offers tips for effective evangelistic Bible studies.

arge numbers of people have become Christians through peer group discussions of the Bible. And when unchurched participants become serious about the Christian faith, they normally begin attending church — often the church of their group's initiator.

Whole churches have been built using this method, and the gospel has penetrated neighborhoods and workplaces that likely would not have opened up to other evangelistic strategies.

What are the keys that make these groups succeed, causing the local church to grow? Here are five:

A "Safe" Invitation

Instead of being asked to "join" a Bible study, people are invited to a home to hear about an idea: a discussion Bible study group for adults who aren't experts. After dessert and coffee, the host or hostess explains how the group will function, using the method of inductive (investigative) study. A twenty-minute sampler — one incident from the gospel of Mark — gives a taste of what's ahead. Those interested set a time and place to start studying Mark 1.

The same thing can happen on the job. Meeting on neutral territory is less threatening for newcomers than meeting in a church. Lunch-hour groups currently meet every week among business people on Wall Street, research scientists at a pharmaceutical corporation, and executives and clerical workers at a chemical firm. There's also an after-work study among garage mechanics with their Christian employer, and breakfast studies (weekday or Saturday) among small-town tradesmen and professionals. Workers who know one another through their jobs but meet in homes range from lobstermen on an island off the Maine coast to astronauts and their spouses in Houston.

Protecting Those New to the Bible

An ideal ratio is six to eight people studying the Bible for the first time with only one or two firm Christians. Groups with too many "experts" do not appeal to raw beginners.

A group of six to ten is large enough to stimulate interaction and new ideas but small enough to let everyone speak and respond to the comments of others. If a group is twelve or larger, the discussion tends to split into two or three competing conversations. The moderator has to exert strong control and may be tempted to lecture. The quiet people and those who know the least sit back. Sometimes they stop coming.

But when everyone has a fair chance, each participant is greatly influenced by what *he* discovers and shares with the group. What he hears himself saying about Jesus' claims will be remembered long after he forgets what someone else tells him. We recall only 20 percent of what we hear but 70 percent of what we say. That's why *discussion* Bible studies are powerful agents of change.

Studying Whole Books of the Bible

Newcomers to the Bible need to lay a foundation before they can handle studies that skip around. Using selected verses here and there to present the gospel message confuses the person who cannot set them into a meaningful context. They also put the person at risk when approached by a cult using a thematic presentation. If methods are similar, the biblically untaught person has a hard time distinguishing between what is authentic and what is counterfeit.

Those new to Bible study should start with Mark; it's clear, concise, full of action, and does not require familiarity with the Old Testament. No wonder missionary translators usually begin with Mark.

Well-prepared Questions

Groups function best with questions that help them observe, interpret, and apply what they find in the Bible text. The questions should be forthright enough to allow each person to take a turn as moderator, moving the group paragraph by paragraph through a chapter. The material must not assume that everyone understands Christian jargon or can easily comprehend a religious mind-track.

Operating Guidelines

The following ground rules protect a group against misuse of Scripture:

1. *Confine the discussion to the chapter being studied.* This keeps the newcomers at equal advantage. As the weeks go by, of course, everyone's scope of knowledge enlarges, and the group is able to refer back to chapters previously studied.

2. *Expect everyone to be responsible for pulling the group back from digressions.* The moderator's job is greatly eased if others in the group help say, "We've gotten onto a tangent. Let's get back to the chapter."

3. *Agree that the document (Mark, for example) will be the authority for the discussion.* People should not be coerced into believing the Bible, but they can be encouraged to be honest about what it says and to refrain from rewriting it. As a group

774 20

continues to study week after week, most members come to recognize the Bible as authoritative.

These guidelines keep a group on the path of orthodoxy. It's difficult to promote heresy in a group studying a book of the Bible in context.

Not every church member should attempt an outreach Bible study. A wise pastor will not try to get "the whole church" into this approach to evangelism. Some Christians tend to tell others too much too soon. The discussion approach requires patience and a willingness to let the non-Christian build a framework of Bible knowledge and discover Christ's claims for himself.

But once this has happened, the person is much more likely to hear and believe a gospel presentation from the pulpit or a Christian friend.

For those the church wants to encourage in this kind of outreach, a preparation series of four or five Wednesday nights or an all-day Saturday workshop may be used. Such a training program should include:

- an explanation of inductive study,
- instruction in sensitivity to the non-Christian,
- practice in introducing the idea of a Bible study to friends and colleagues,
- participation in an actual Bible study discussion.

Copies of the study questions for Mark should be available as well. (For a handbook, *How to Start a Neighborhood Bible Study*, and study guides, write Neighborhood Bible Studies, Box 2221, Dobbs Ferry, NY 10522.)

At one such workshop, two men were role-playing the initial invitation. Jim later reported, "When Charlie asked me how I'd like to 'join a group and study the Word of God,' he lost me. I was suddenly aware that a person who had never studied the Bible would not call it 'the Word of God.' It would have been better if he'd simply asked me if I'd like to be in a Bible study for nonexperts. I would have said yes to that."

Outreach can start in a neighborhood with one or two young mothers from the church inviting women on their block. The daytime group becomes so valuable that they want their husbands to share the experience, and an evening couples' Bible study begins. Next, business men and women start studies at work.

Those who come to Christ through a discussion Bible study are able to reach out to their friends in the same way. Meanwhile, church members mature spiritually and become more effective leaders in the church. Small-group Bible study is a ministry multiplier.

E I G H T

CLOSING THE EVANGELISTIC BACK DOOR

Most Protestant congregations . . . find it easier to receive new members than to assimilate them into the fellowship and to help these new members gain a sense of belonging.

LYLE SCHALLER

They broke bread in their homes and ate together with glad and sincere hearts, praising God and enjoying the favor of all the people. And the Lord added to their number daily those who were being saved.

ACTS 2:46–47

Even churches with effective evangelism still face a common frustration: many people who enter the church through the front door leave soon after through the church's "back door," usually without telling anyone in the church why. Win and Charles Arn, the president and director, respectively, of the Institute for American Church Growth in Pasadena, California, studied this problem and learned what's behind it.

Basing their conclusions on extensive research, they examine the two major props that keep that back door open. First appearing several years ago as an article in LEADERSHIP Journal, this chapter received from readers the highest rating in the magazine's history.

The visitation teams headed back to the church at the close of a Thursday evening's work. One group in particular was excited about their call at the home of Tom and Emily Kenyon. After some polite small talk, the conversation had turned to religion. The group leader followed the basic evangelistic outline they had learned and eventually asked whether the Kenyons wouldn't like to make a Christian decision.

Tom and Emily responded affirmatively and prayed the prayer in the booklet. Follow-up material was left with the couple, along with an invitation to attend church the next Sunday. This experience, when shared with the other calling teams, was enough to qualify the entire night of calling as a fine success.

The next Sunday, Tom and Emily Kenyon did indeed attend church. While they didn't know anyone and could not find any of the three who had called that Thursday night, they tried to be friendly and enter into the Sunday morning activities. They attended the church once more two weeks later. It was their last visit. A phone call from the church, following up on their earlier decision, was met with a polite but noncommittal response. The Kenyons had just left through the "evangelistic back door."

What happened? Why did these apparently genuine Christian decisions not proceed naturally into church involvement and continued growth? Why do many modern evangelistic endeavors have similar dropout patterns? In talking with pastors and church leaders across the nation, we have found that the evangelistic back door is, indeed, very large and very well used.

Some Clues

Research is now demonstrating that the *process* by which people arrive at a point of Christian decision is a key factor in whether they become responsible members or drop out. The effect of the evangelistic process on the eventual results is so significant, in fact, that it can be predicted *which decision makers* will grow into responsible church members within the first year and which will become inactive. What is particularly discomforting is that many churches and parachurch groups today use methods that actually *increase* the likelihood of new converts' never becoming active church members.

The bottom line for evaluating the success of any evangelistic effort must be "Did those who made a Christian profession become part of the church?" To an increasing number of church leaders, successful evangelism is no longer "How many decisions were made?" or "How many came forward?" or "How many phoned in to accept Christ?" Faithful response to the Great Commission is achieved when the evangelistic process, under the Holy Spirit's guidance, produces actual, factual growth in the church — growth that is measurable in one year and five — growth that reproduces itself in new disciples.

When this goal is not achieved, well-intentioned but usually inaccurate excuses are given:

"They didn't understand their commitment."

"Our follow-up program was lacking."

"There were no other people in the church their age."

"The results are up to God."

But research is now showing clearly that the more fundamental cause of this high "infant mortality rate" lies upstream in the actual evangelistic process. In closing the evangelistic back door, two key areas produce significant increases in lasting disciples and growing churches. The first is *process*; the second concerns *ratios*.

The Process

What is it about many current evangelistic methods that is so counterproductive to the goal?

1. *A manipulative process tends to create dropouts.* It is possible to sort evangelism methods and approaches three ways:

Informative transmission sees evangelism as a one-way communication of certain facts the hearer needs to know. When the information is correctly presented, an appropriate decision can be expected. The relationship between the evangelizer and the prospect is like that of teacher and student, the goal being to impart certain correct information. Thus, the bottom line is "How many people heard the message?"

Another approach to evangelism may be called the *manipulative monologue*. It may center on an emotional appeal or use a set of carefully prepared questions. The relationship between the believer and the nonbeliever more closely resembles a salesman and a customer, the perceived goal being to close the sale. The bottom line in this view is "How many people said yes?"

The third approach, *nonmanipulative dialogue*, views evangelism as a two-way process of honest interaction. The assumption is that not all people see things the same way, and one canned approach will not be appropriate in every situation. Evangelism is an effort to respond to the other person as an individual and portray the value of the Christian faith in terms of individualized needs. The relationship between Christian and non-Christian in this case is friend to friend, the goal being to express an honest concern for the other.

In *The Pastor's Church Growth Handbook, Volume II*, Flavil Yeakley reports on a study of how church members view the evangelistic process and the results of their evangelistic endeavors. The study identified three groups (240 people each) of "recipients" of an evangelistic presentation: (1) those who made a Christian commitment and are now actively involved in a local church; (2) those who made a commitment but soon dropped out; and (3) those who said, "No, thanks." Here are the startling results:

Seventy percent (169 of 240) of those who are now active members came to Christ and their church as the result of a member who saw evangelism as nonmanipulative dialogue. By contrast, 87 percent (209) of those now *in*active came to their point of decision through a member who used manipulative monologue. And of those who said, "No, thanks," to an evangelistic presentation, 75 percent (180) did so in response to a would-be persuader who saw evangelism as a process of communicating certain facts, content, and theology. Partial results from this study:

How They View Evangelism

Categories of subjects	Information Transmission	Manipulative Monologue	Nonmanipulative Dialogue	Totals
Converts— Now Active Members	35	36	169	240
Dropouts	25	209	6	240
Nonconverts	180	58	2	240

The corollary: Effective evangelistic training and strategy encourage a view of nonmanipulative dialogue between Christians and non-Christians.

2. *An evangelistic process that sees its goal as a "decision" rather than a "disciple" tends to create dropouts.*

When the goal is a "soul saved," God's plan for making disciples is often short-circuited. The fact is that not all deciders become disciples; the two are not synonymous. The biblical goal is not simply an oral confession but a life transformed and a participating member of Christ's body. Nowhere in Scripture is the word *decision* found — yet the word *disciple* appears again and again.

The corollary: Effective evangelism sees disciple making as a process, not an event. A "decision" is only one element of many in the goal of seeing people become disciples and responsible church members.

3. *An evangelistic process that presents the gospel one time and then asks for a response tends to create dropouts.* We all know stories of people who heard the Good News once, were gloriously changed, and went on to become great men or women of faith. When these miraculous events happen — and they do — we can rejoice. It should be understood, however, that this is unusual, not the norm. More often when someone comes to faith, that person has heard the message *again and again and again*, then makes a Christian commitment.

A person may hear the gospel in a Bible study class. He may hear it through music. He may see the Christian life demonstrated in the lives of friends. He may hear a testimony at a church social event. He may read it in Scripture, a tract, or a book. He may hear it on radio or television. Then, after many exposures, a season of receptivity comes into that person's life — a time of need — when the seed that has been sown breaks into new life, takes root, sprouts, and grows.

Research underscores this fact. In comparing active and inactive members, Yeakley found (in *Why Churches Grow*) that those who continued as active church members had been exposed to an average of 5.79 different Christian influences *prior* to their commitment. The dropouts, by comparison, had seen or heard the Christian message only 2.16 times before their decision.

As an evangelistic strategy, the more times a person is exposed to the gospel message prior to a Christian commitment, the more likely he or she is to understand the implications of that commitment. The fewer the exposures prior to commitment, the greater the likelihood of dropping out.

The corollary: Effective evangelistic strategy seeks to expose potential disciples to many and varied presentations of the gospel.

4. *An evangelistic process that does not build relationships with the local church, its programs, and its ministry tends to create dropouts.* When the events leading up to a non-Christian's profession of faith occur outside any relationship with the people of the local chruch, no ties are established, and the perceived need for involvement in the church is low. This may be true not only when decisions are made in large crusades or via mass media, but even when evangelism calls are made from a local church.

When the new Christian has not built any friendships with members in the church, has not become part of any group where there is a sense of belonging, and has not had prior exposure to the church, its people, its beliefs, and its expectations, some large roadblocks are put in the path of assimilation.

What should a disciple-making strategy include to remove this deficiency in most evangelistic methods? The strategy should seek to foster genuine caring relationships between a *variety* of members and the potential disciple. It should also seek to involve the potential disciple in several appropriate groups and church programs where new friendships can be made. The more exposures a non-Christian can have to the person of Christ through his people and the church, the more complete his or her understanding of Christ and his love.

The New Testament compares the healthy functioning of the church body to the human body. Arms, legs, eyes, and ears come together as parts of the body. Each member has certain gifts and abilities, and not all members have the same gifts. Because of this, the whole more accurately reflects the person of Christ than any of its parts in isolation. One member brings strengths where another may be weak. Some members are able to relate to a special need of a non-Christian or unchurched person better than others. And in the process, evangelism moves from a few lone rangers to a total team effort. Then, when a Christian commitment is made, it is founded on experience with the body and a growing understanding of what this new commitment means.

The corollary: The closer evangelism is to the local church, the greater the fruit that remains.

Crucial Ratios

While the *process* of a person's becoming a disciple and responsible church member is one key element to a successful Great Commission strategy, a second element, equally important, focuses on the church environment into which that new Christian is entering. It concerns *ratios* in the church.

Here are seven ratios that have significant effect in closing the evangelistic back door:

1. *Friendship ratio* — *1:7.* Each new person should be able to identify at least seven friends in the church within the first six months.

Friendships appear to be the strongest bond cementing new members to their congregation. If they do not immediately develop meaningful friendships in their church, expect them to return to their old friendships — and ways — outside the church. Seven new friendships are a minimum; ten, fifteen, or more are better.

The time factor is important as well. The first six months are crucial. New people not integrated into the body within that period are well on their way out the back door. The following chart clearly illustrates the importance of establishing friendships in the church during the first six months. Note that all fifty "converts — now active members" could name three or more friends in the church, with thirteen new members identifying seven, twelve identifying eight, and twelve listing nine or more. The "dropouts" show almost the opposite pattern in the new friendships they did, or more correctly did not, establish in their churches.

Number of New Friends in the Church within Six Months	0	1	2	3	4	5	6	7	8	9+	Total
Converts—Now Active Members	0	0	0	1	2	2	8	13	12	12	50
Dropouts	8	13	14	8	4	2	1	0	0	0	50

2. Role/Task Ratio — 60:100. At least 60 roles and tasks should be available for every 100 members in a church.

A role or task means a specific function or responsibility (choir, committee member, teacher, officer, etc.). Typical churches of 300 members have no more than 80 roles and tasks available. Of those 80 roles/tasks, 60 are filled by 30 people (the willing workers with more than one job). The remaining 20 roles and tasks are filled by an additional 20 people, thus involving 50 out of 300 members. Would such a typical church have a place for Tom and Emily to find meaningful responsibility? Probably not.

The lack of variety and number of roles/tasks/ministries in most churches creates an environment that actually *produces* inactive members. Such a church of 300 needs to open itself to newcomers by creating at least 100 new roles and tasks — not busy-work but "kingdom work," "Great Commission work," ministries that focus on meeting needs and changing lives.

These kinds of roles are often called "Class II roles." Whereas "Class I roles" focus primarily inward toward maintenance of the existing institution, Class II roles focus primarily outward toward the surrounding community in an effort to reach persons for Christ and the church. Most plateaued or declining churches average fifteen Class I roles to every Class II role. A more productive ratio would be 3:1 (for every three

Class I roles, at least one Class II role). While this is more of an outreach ratio than an assimilation ratio, it does give an important clue to the priority of the church and, thus, the probable reception given to the newcomer.

3. *Group Ratio — 7:100.* At least seven relational groups — places where friendships are built — should be available in a church for every 100 members.

In studying churches involved in our institute's Two-Year Growth Process, we have found that plateaued and declining churches fall far short of this group-to-member ratio. The consequence of too few groups for members to build meaningful relationships is a high rate of inactives using the back door. Good questions to ask are "How many groups does our church have per 100 members?" "What percentage of the congregation is a regular part of one or more groups?" "How many new converts/new members have become a regular part of such groups in the last two years?" "How many have not?"

Creating an effective group life is a fundamental building block for growth and incorporation. This important ratio is affirmed by other authorities. Lyle Schaller writes in *Assimilating New Members*, "It usually is necessary to have six or seven of these groups. . .for each one hundred members who are thirteen or fourteen years of age or older."

This ratio in a church will provide important answers to the question "How open is this church to newcomers?"

4. *New-Group Ratio — 1:5.* Of every five relational groups in a church, one should have been started in the past two years.

The reason new groups are important is that established groups usually reach a saturation point sometime between nine and eighteen months after their formation. When a group has reached this saturation zone, in most cases it stops growing and no longer assimilates new people. Two or three members may leave and two or three may fill their places, but for all practical purposes, the group remains plateaued.

How do you know when a group has reached the saturation point? You make a graph. If a group has not grown in the last six months, it has probably reached saturation.

One remedy is simply to form new groups, with new people involved. This provides for continued freshness in the group life of a congregation. It decreases the number of inactives. It helps close the evangelistic back door.

5. *Committee Member Ratio — 1:5.* One of every five committee members should have joined the church within the last two years.

In conversation with the pastor of an old-line church in the Pacific Northwest, I asked, "How long would I need to be a member of the church before I might be elected to office?"

He studied my question for a moment, then asked, "Would you attend regularly, give faithfully, and exemplify the Christian life?"

"Yes," I responded.

"Then you would be elected to office sometime between the twelfth and fourteenth year after you joined."

No wonder this church has a terminal illness! New board and committee members bring fresh and exciting ideas, along with vitality. They are positive and enthusiastic about their new church, ready to earn their sense of belonging. They provide the best source of volunteers.

A regular review of the boards and committees in a church to assure the 1:5 ratio will encourage an openness in the power structure and assure that the church never forgets its real mission.

6. *Staff ratio — 1:150.* A church should have one full-time staff member for every 150 persons in worship.

This ratio is a good indicator of a church's commitment to growth. If the ratio reaches 1:225–250, it is unusual to see any significant increase in active membership. While more persons may join the church, the evangelistic back door will open wider. Adding a staff person *before* this point is reached helps a church anticipate the influx of new persons and provides a church environment to accommodate them. Here is the rule of thumb:

Average Worship Attendance	Full-time Staff	Half-time Staff
0–150	1	
150–200	1	1
200–300	2	
300–400	2	1
400–500	3	
500–600	3	1

We suggest the first person added after the pastor be hired to minister full-time in the area of evangelism and church growth, including the incorporation of new members into the fellowship. This person will normally pay for himself or herself through new giving units added to the church within the first year and a half. In some churches we have worked with, the new staff person's salary was paid within nine months.

7. *Visitor Ratio — 3:10.* Of the first-time visitors who live in the church's ministry area, three of every ten should be actively involved within a year.

Calculating the visitor ratio provides three insights into a church's attitude toward newcomers: (1) it indicates the present members' *openness* to visitors; (2) it indicates the *priority* of visitors in the functioning of the church; and (3) it indicates the effectiveness of the church's *follow-up strategy*.

Whether persons are transferring to a new church or trying their first church, as Tom and Emily were, they always visit before joining. Visitors are the *only* source of new members (except for the children of believers). If visitors do not feel genuinely welcome, needed, and wanted, they seldom return. Our studies indicate that through an effective strategy, some churches are seeing four of every ten local visitors come back a second time. An incorporation strategy that focuses on these second-time visitors will result in 70–75 percent of them joining within a year (hence the 3:10 ratio of first-time local visitors joining within a year).

The typical nongrowing church, on the other hand, sees

only 10–12 percent of its first-time visitors join. Such a percentage, it turns out, is almost the exact number a church can expect to lose each year through transfer, death, and falling away.

We Can Do Better

It is important that the relatively high mortality rate from some present-day evangelistic methods not come to be viewed as normal or unavoidable. With adequate training and appropriate methods, churches can see a significantly greater harvest.

Is there really any value in investing time, energy, money, and people in the work of evangelism only to see the hard-won results drop away? Closing the evangelistic back door is possible. We *can* see more-lasting results if we begin viewing evangelism and incorporation as two sides of one coin, interdependent, both essential for the growth of God's church.

Most churches can substantially increase their effectiveness in making disciples and responsible church members. Let's slam the back door.

NINE

WHAT NEW CHRISTIANS NEED MOST

It's a strange and tragic truth that spiritual things can be unlearned.

ART GLASSER

People, like trees, must grow or die. There's no standing still.

JOSEPH SHORE

Once you bring a baby into the world, you've got to raise it till it's ready to fend for itself. But what's the best way? There are as many methods as there are child psychologists, from Spock to Dobson and everything in between. Choosing the right approach is one of a parent's biggest responsibilities.

In the same way, once people have been won to Christ, the local church has the responsibility to help them mature. But churches differ in their approaches to meeting this need. Which methods are most effective, and what are the keys to making them work? Dean Merrill, formerly senior editor of LEADERSHIP *and now editor of* **Christian Herald** *magazine, explores three common approaches.*

Have you noticed that the most essential parts of a process are often the most complicated?

It is far easier for an architect to sketch a dashing roof line than to work out the tedious schematics. It is always more fun to invite guests for dinner than to cook the meal and do the dishes afterward.

In ministry, when we invite a person to follow Christ and the answer is yes, there's a surge of rejoicing all around. Darkness has given way to light; a new life has begun. The next stage, however — the crucial stage if this spiritual newborn is to survive — is the developing, forming, nurturing, establishing, rooting, confirming, and discipling of the new Christian.

As the previous sentence illustrates, we in the church use varying language to describe the task. But there is no question about the importance. From the moment Jesus stared down his most impetuous disciple and said, "Feed my lambs," the value of caring for the spiritually young has been set. Church leaders agree that answering an evangelist's public call is not enough. Becoming a member is not enough. Without subsequent feeding, the act of beginning becomes a dead end.

We cringe as we eavesdrop on John Wesley storming at his preachers, "How dare you lead people to Christ without providing adequate opportunity for growth and nurture! Anything less is simply begetting children for the murderer."

And in our own time, we affirm Lyle Schaller's premise that "it is not Christian to invite a person to unite with a specific congregation and then not accept that person into the fellowship of that congregation."

The Daunting Task

Yet the task looms so large, so intangible, that we aren't immediately sure where it starts, and especially where it finishes. What does it take to bring a person to spiritual maturity? What stages of growth can we anticipate? How do we guide the new Christian from A to B to C? Do we ever reach a point where we can quit?

Any parent knows the peculiar sinking feeling that hits, often within days or weeks of bringing the firstborn home from the hospital. The celebration quiets down, the grandparents say good-by, and in the silence late at night you're suddenly struck with the awesomeness of what it means to raise a child to adulthood.

It's up to us to do and be everything this new little life needs from now on. Yes, there's a pediatrician to consult (for a fee), and miscellaneous friends and relatives with free advice, and later on a school system to help educate. But the buck stops right here, for better or for worse, in sickness and in health, till independence do us part.

As philosopher Michael Novak says, "The raising of children . . . brings each of us breathtaking vistas of our inadequacy."

The rearing of spiritual offspring is, if anything, even more intimidating, since indicators are less tangible (no height-and-weight charts, no report cards) and our chances to do our work are scant compared to the twenty-four hours a day natural parents have. We all carry dreams of what we hope for: the eager, committed, young Christian who devours the Scriptures on a daily basis, begins changing his or her lifestyle to match what is read, participates fervently in public worship, seeks out a place of service in the church, prays freely and sees answers to those prayers, and speaks openly of his new allegiance to Christ without embarrassment.

But deep within, we know such pleasant results are not guaranteed, and if they fail to materialize, we assume it will be more our fault than anyone else's.

So we mull over our parenting strategies. Is it better to jar the new Christian with a sense of all-things-new? Should we meet several times a week and require homework, for example? Or does that seem cultish? Shall we rather set an easy stride (after all, these are adults) and keep things comfortable?

A wide difference of opinion exists not only on the level of intensity, but also on where to begin. Some churches are firmly of the "learn and grow first, then serve" philosophy, while others lean strongly toward on-the-job training.

What follows are descriptions of three different "ways to raise a baby." None would claim to be the only way. From these accounts, church leaders can study, imagine, and pick and choose in order "to prepare God's people for works of service, so that the body of Christ may be built up until we all . . . become mature, attaining to the whole measure of the fulness of Christ" (Eph. 4:12–13).

One Friend to Another

West Valley Christian Church in Canoga Park, California, is not one of southern California's megachurches. It began in 1976 under the leadership of church planter Glenn Kirby and is now a congregation of four hundred. Single-family homes surround the church on three sides; to the west lies a public school playground.

West Valley's emphasis on helping new Christians grow emerged almost unintentionally. The church has had a private school almost from the beginning, and it was the first school administrator who "kept after the rest of us about the need to give people some kind of big-picture approach to the Bible," says Kirby. "He put together some material, and we went through it as a staff. Later on, I revised it, and in January 1980, we offered our 'Bible History Overview' for the first time in the adult Sunday school classes."

Kirby was not yet to the point of thinking specifically about new believers. He and Gary Olsby, then minister of Christian education, simply wanted to give members a handle on the big, thick, black Book. So they spent nine months going from Genesis through to the early spread of the church, helping people understand who lived where and who preceded whom. Were members turned off by this large a dose of history?

"Most Christians don't have the story line in their heads," says Kirby. "They got excited as they began to acquire the overview." Sunday school attendance, in fact, went from 150 to 210 during those nine months.

What next? Specifically, how could newcomers to the church get the same foundation? It was at this point that a Laubach-style "each one teach one" concept entered Glenn Kirby's mind. Before long, he and Olsby boiled down the course to a blue, 61-page workbook, complete with maps, charts, and fill-in-the-blanks. The nine-month class became a set of thirteen (and later eight) lessons for informal use.

"We asked how many graduates of our Sunday school class would be willing to reteach the same material — not to a roomful, but to one or two others in their homes," Olsby remembers. "That sounded easy enough, and fifty people said yes."

So they were put to work. Many of them gathered their own students: friends or neighbors who responded affirmatively to the question, "My church has this eight-week Bible History Overview course; would you like for me to take you through it? We could even do it at your house if you like." Those who lacked prospects were matched with recent visitors to the church or others who wanted to brush up on the Bible.

The course is a simple who-what-when-where. It does not attempt to cover the Old Testament's Wisdom Literature or the writings of the prophets. Nor does it tackle the New Testament Epistles. It simply lays out a parade of people who walked with God (Enoch, Noah, Abraham . . .) and another parade of those who didn't (Jereboam, Manasseh . . .), showing the advantages of the first over the second.

Week by week, in homes across the valley, interesting things began to happen. Some had more to do with evangelism than discipleship or Christian education. Rod and Rita White led five separate studies, four of which resulted in conversions and baptisms. One couple they touched were the Setsers.

"When Bonny and I came to West Valley," says Bob Setser, "the Holy Spirit had just begun to make us aware of our spiritual needs. Bonny came from a totally nonreligious home, and I'd turned away from the church in my late teens. But we both felt a void in our lives and wondered if the Lord could fill it. After a few visits, Glenn Kirby asked if we'd like to do an overview study of the Bible with another couple as teachers. We agreed, and that's how we met Rod and Rita. Over the next several months as the historical panorama of God's plan was explained, the combination of the Holy Spirit's work plus Rod and Rita's guidance and testimony convinced us we were on the right track. Before we completed the study, we asked Jesus into our lives."

Subsequently, the Setsers became teachers of the overview, and *their* first students, the Paladinos, also joined the church. The network of influence has by this time become extensive.

"This course *was* our evangelism program for several years," the ministers remember. Now West Valley has developed a calling program and some other outreaches, but the overview continues to draw people toward a Christian commitment. The eighth week specifically stresses Peter's appeal to the crowd at Pentecost (Acts 2:38), and the workbook says, "To become a Christian today, we should do the same things these people did." This is often the point of conversion for those who haven't reached it earlier.

After seven weeks of learning and informal conversation, this decision is not as threatening. "Sometimes a student may feel lost or be very shy," says Olsby, "and initially the teacher must do all the talking. Other times a student can't read very well, and the teacher must do all the reading from Scripture. But most sessions are a free-flowing discussion with plenty of time for personal questions."

West Valley has since added a second course (taught mainly in Sunday school) that looks much like what other churches use *first*. "Basic Teachings of the Christian Faith" has eight lessons on prayer, the church, service, sharing your faith, dealing with temptation, and church history. A third course on spiritual gifts includes a diagnostic questionnaire to help people identify their gifts and put them to use.

"Eventually, we want all our members to go through all three courses," says Kirby. "Together they take a beginning person from salvation through to grounding in the faith and on to serving."

The church is now using the one-to-one concept to try to accelerate older Christians' spiritual growth. The elders and ministers meet in pairs each week for sixty-to-ninety-minute sessions emphasizing accountability. Partners set specific weekly goals (pray with my wife five times; memorize a portion of Scripture) and pray for each other. The following week, they compare how close they came to reaching their goals. Kirby and current minister of Christian education Steve Hancock hope to have all members in these long-term partnerships eventually. That's likely; through the Bible History Overview, West Valley members have grown accustomed to a close, one-to-one approach.

"I admit we're tempted sometimes to form more groups rather than keep finding teachers for one-to-one sessions,"

Kirby says. "But we feel we'd be giving up too many bene-fits." Among them:

— More and more people gain experience teaching.

— New teachers overcome their fears, because they're already familiar with the material and can simply follow the workbook.

— The new believer builds a solid, close relationship with an experienced Christian.

— People are grounded in the flow of Bible history from Creation to the church.

— Instructors model how to live the Christian life and how to study the Bible, two keys to discipleship.

— It builds bridges into the church.

And the bonus is this: It seems to generate more Christians along the way.

Mainstreaming

A second approach to nurturing new believers might be called "mainstreaming," to borrow a bit of jargon from the educational world. In recent years, many school administrators have backed away from the earlier practice of segregating students with special needs or handicaps. Instead of filling up special classrooms with atypical students, they have tried placing as many as possible in the same rooms with "normal" students, for two reasons: (1) to surround them with examples of what "normalcy" is, and (2) to heighten sensitivity among ordinary students for those with special needs.

Some church leaders are taking a similar approach to new Christians. Having set an environment that says, "We are Christians in process, and we all have a lot to learn," they guide new believers into the mainstream of congregational learning as quickly as possible, with a minimum of special attention.

One such church is Peninsula Bible Church in Palo Alto, California. The church is not as massive architecturally as many readers of the book *Body Life* and others by Ray Stedman, pastor, might have imagined. Packed into the middle of a block, with less than 150 feet of frontage, the plain, 1,000-seat auditorium extends back toward parking lots that hide behind adjacent houses. A one-lane driveway snakes along one side of the building and empties out on the other. "We're as far as we can go on this property," says Paul Winslow, a staff pastor since 1972, "but God provided a second building (seating 450) in Cupertino, ten miles south."

So Peninsula Bible Church has taken to providing five Sunday services, two at one location, three at another. It has also parceled its pastors out all over the peninsula, with encouragement to develop the body of Christ not just at 3505 Middlefield Road, but throughout the region, from San Jose to the edge of San Francisco. More importantly, the leadership has honed a precise self-definition.

"We're a church that ministers to believers," says Winslow, choosing his words carefully. "The nonbeliever is never addressed corporately here; we don't have revival meetings or altar calls, for example. All the evangelism happens 'out there,' in the world. And believe me, there's plenty to do; we're only forty miles from San Francisco, what many say is the most evil city in the world. Our area is also incredibly affluent: more Porsches and Mercedeses per capita here than in Germany. Stanford University is less than two miles away.

"How do we affect this peninsula for Christ? We've decided to pour all our efforts into maturing and equipping the believers. We're not a center for evangelism but for teaching. Our goal is not for people to be won by the professional pastors but by the regular Christians — they're the evangelizers. And when they lead someone to the Lord, they don't hand them over to PBC for follow-up care. They involve them in the same processes that helped them grow when they were new Christians."

Thus, the Sunday meetings are consistently geared to a single purpose: exposition of the Word. When Stedman, Winslow, or one of the others steps to the pulpit, he means to do one thing only: unfold and apply a passage of Scripture. One gets a glimpse of this when walking in the church's front entrance: two imposing racks line the narthex walls from floor to ceiling, with slots for as many as a thousand different "Discovery Papers" — transcripts of past messages. A thirty-page index lists available titles. New Christians along with all the rest are surrounded by this abundance of Bible teaching.

On weeknights, Discovery Seminars are held at the church: two-hour classes that require tuition and run the gamut from "Friendly Toward Jesus?" (Peninsula's sole accommodation to new Christians, offered spring term only) to "Modern Church History" to classes on hermeneutics. Other electives covering books of Scripture are offered on Sunday morning, although space is a constraint.

"The whole church gravitates toward studying and applying the Bible — it's in the air," says Winslow. "If you don't enjoy that, you start to feel uncomfortable here. We don't have enough of the other usual trappings — a large music program, gymnasium, or social activities, for example — to hold you. You get bored if you don't get into the Word."

One reason this works at Peninsula Bible is that its Silicon Valley constituency is highly educated, eager to read and learn for themselves. They take notes during the preaching, snap up the Discovery Papers on their way out, and may stop to buy a book in the church bookstore.

Not everyone, of course, can find his own way to grow. Pastor Ron Ritchie, who ministers to singles each Sunday in the upstairs room of the Menu Tree Restaurant in Mountain View, knows the difficulty.

"Sometimes I'll wake up at three in the morning," he says, "and the Lord will say to me, 'Ron, where's Bill?' Then I remember I haven't seen him in a while; he's fallen through the cracks. I look him up as soon as I can and give some personal attention.

"In that sense, caring for the new Christian is the responsibility of us all," he continues. "There's no program, no delegation. But if you find the Lord at PBC — and don't move out of the area — I can guarantee there will be more 'food' than you can eat. That's our whole purpose as a church."

What are the pros and cons of mainstreaming as a way to care for the spiritually young?

Its advantages are that it sweeps up new Christians in a mass movement of sorts, a large band of pilgrims all headed the same direction. They aren't made to feel a breed apart, rookies to be given unusual treatment. They quickly rub shoulders with Christians of all types and experience, learning what they can from a multitude of sources.

Such an approach largely dismisses questions about sequence. If you happen to drop in at the point where Ray Stedman is in the eleventh week of 2 Corinthians, that's just the way it is. The Word is alive in all its parts, and nothing will be harmful for you; the Spirit can be trusted to guide you and personalize the message as needed. Eventually, all the bases will be covered.

Some church leaders will endorse the previous paragraph, while others will not. All can probably agree that mainstreaming *does* require a sizable amount of weekly Bible presentation *with practical application*, else the bases will not be covered for a long time, and new Christians may falter. Certainly mainstreaming should not be viewed as an easy way out, and its best practitioners do not do so in the least. Their desire is rather to keep from overcomplicating the new life in Christ, to make it as natural and as accessible as possible.

The Short Course

Many churches include some kind of brief, church-based orientation class in their overall ministry to new Christians. We turn now to those for whom such a class is the prime element.

"When you finally get up the courage to try church — and you haven't been there in years — it's scary," says Don Bubna, former pastor of Salem (Oregon) Alliance Church. "Every human being has at least some tinge of fear at being rejected by a new group. You might manage sitting through a morning worship service all right, but beyond that, you're not at all sure you'll survive."

That's why Bubna created "The Welcome Class," a free-wheeling, no-demand "guided happening"every Sunday morning, year round. The only qualification to attend: you had to be a newcomer or visitor to the church. People were welcome to stay as long as they wished, although they'd notice after three months that the topics started to recycle. It was their special zone in which to relax, breathe, laugh, find out what the Christian life is about, get close to the church's leadership, and begin to put down roots.

Bubna got the technique down to a science. He first experimented with it while pastoring a small church in San Diego in the early sixties. When he went to Salem, the class became a permanent fixture. As of this writing, 80 percent of the eleven hundred people who regularly attend Salem Alliance have gone through this portal. Bubna calls it "the single most significant contributor to two decades of growth."

A typical morning would begin with thirty-five to fifty people entering the pastor's study (actually a large classroom that he enjoyed throughout the week in order to host the Welcome Class on Sundays). There they found an incomplete sentence on the chalkboard: "You would know me better if ____ " "Some of the best advice I ever had was ____ " or "Something I learned from a tough experience was ____ ." (On some Sundays, people were given the option of asking anything about the church's practices or beliefs.)

While thinking of your answer, the pastor, his wife, or associate teacher Darrel Dixon would put a cup of coffee or tea into your hand and introduce you to someone else nearby. Soon the session began with the gregarious pastor saying, "I'm Don Bubna, and you're the Welcome Class. This is a gathering of new people and visitors who meet each week to discuss things Christians commonly believe.

"It's a place where people are important. That's why we take time each week for each of you to introduce yourself. The open-ended statement on the board will also let you tell us a little more about yourself — if you want to. You may complete it seriously, humorously, philosophically — or just pass. Who wants to be first?"

Often one of the leadership team broke the ice, being careful not to sound too theological. Soon the comments were flowing freely, and if somebody said he was from Spokane, others were welcome to find out whether he knew their cousin who lived there. It was common for someone to spill the news of a sick child, a job loss, or a family concern. Would the person like prayer about that? Someone was promptly invited to lead out.

Then came the Scripture for the day, with Bibles handed out for those who needed them. Bubna did not assume people knew how to find Psalms or Acts; he guided them by saying things like "about three quarters of the way back in the book." Everyone read the text silently and then framed a comment about it. There was no lecture waiting to be unleashed, however. The teaching was done via discovery, with plenty of give-and-take and frequent life application.

Says Tom Riordan, a lapsed Catholic whose wife talked him into attending in late 1983, "The format was essentially educational, but it worked on such an intimate level that at times it was, for me, really moving. I would get caught up in what was happening, and the more I opened up, the more I gained." He eventually came to realize his commitment to Christ was still unformed, and Don Bubna led him to solid commitment in a restaurant the following March.

Tucked away in Bubna's notes, of course, was an agenda. "We were teaching basic Bible doctrine, but we never called it that." The five areas to be covered: Scripture, God, our human predicament, Jesus Christ, and the church — what it means to be the people of God. The last topic took as much time as the other four put together.

Sometimes the Bible study wrapped up early, leaving time for general questions such as "Share one thing you've been learning about God," "Tell us where you are in your pilgrimage of faith," or "What were the circumstances that surrounded your coming to commitment to Christ?"

Certain logistics are important, says Bubna:

1. The right location. He feels the pastor's study carries a certain sense of privilege to it that attracts some people.

2. The presence of the church's preaching pastor and his wife. "New people want some kind of identification with them. This also provides personal contact with those who most likely will merge into the congregation before long."

3. A solid associate teacher to provide continuity when the pastor must be out of town. Darrel Dixon had been on the scene in the Welcome Class for more than ten years.

4. A visiting elder each week, who is always introduced. This furthers the exposure of leadership and sets up more relationships.

5. Periodic promotion. Although newcomers might enter the class at any point, special letters of invitation were mailed just ahead of the first Sunday of each quarter to those who had recently signed a friendship pad in the main service. It told them where to find coffee, a sweet roll, and comfortable give-and-take with the pastor next Sunday morning.

The class was also occasionally announced in the bulletin and from the pulpit. But most new people were brought or referred by friends, previous attenders of the class who liked it and wanted others to experience it for themselves. Visitation teams also followed up first-timers with a personal presentation of the gospel in their homes.

Along the way, those who professed faith in Christ were invited to separate baptismal classes, two or three sessions that prepared them to give their public witness at the time of baptism.

Eventually, members moved out of the Welcome Class to other kinds of learning: adult electives, home Bible studies, or intensive, ninety-minute discipling classes on Wednesdays. Yet even these retained the discovery approach, the warmth, and the humor of the Welcome Class. Don Bubna's goal in each structure was to live out the words of Romans 15:7:

"Welcome one another, therefore, as Christ has welcomed you, for the glory of God."

The short-course approach to forming new believers is an easily grasped, conventional strategy, particularly in our current era of adult education. Many North Americans are well conditioned to taking courses in order to learn whatever they want to know. And they give such courses a measure of seriousness.

Such structure tells people there is a body of information to be covered here, enough that it will require more than one sitting. Yet it isn't endless; you can finish on a certain date and feel you've accomplished something.

The class also tells the congregation each week as they read the church schedule in the bulletin that early discipling is going on. It keeps veteran Christians in touch with the fact that, among other things, this church is a continual "nursery."

However, if the class is not more than a class, the new life in Christ can be reduced to gray academics. That's why the style of the "Welcome Class" is especially noteworthy. Bubna worked hard to join fellowship with learning, the heart with the head.

The problem of sequence is not entirely solved. Those who enter midstream end up getting some first things second. That is partly why these are short courses. Students don't have to wait a long time to fill in the missing blanks, and as we have noted before, the question of whether sequence is important is debatable anyway.

The short course, in the end, is neither the most daring nor the most demanding form of nurture for new Christians. But it is practical, manageable, and can be significantly effective.

An Untidy Operation

The one-on-one, mainstreaming, and short-course approaches are just a few of the ways congregations care for the infants in their midst. Some churches use "covenant groups," intense "Timothy-ing" in a small-group setting. Still others rely on a full-blown school, offering an array of courses in the Christian life with professors, credits, and electives. The styles and techniques vary according to pastoral temperaments, congregational strengths, and regional needs.

Perhaps we should accept the fact that forming new Christians will never be a tidy operation. We will always have questions about whether we are doing enough of the right kinds of things. We will probably go on wondering about the proper sequence, or whether sequence matters. We are forced to live with residual levels of uncertainty.

Yet we can take comfort in the thought most pediatricians pass along to anxious parents: "Don't worry quite so much. The kid won't break. With a reasonable amount of love and attention, she'll be fine."

Part of the task of helping new Christians grow is the work of discipleship, working intensely in one-on-one relationships. Yet the pastor's heavy time investment in this process can lead other church members to feel slighted. Thus, in the second part of this chapter, E. Stanley Ott, associate pastor of Covenant Presbyterian Church in West Lafayette, Indiana, describes the keys he has found to discipling individuals without appearing to play favorites in the eyes of the rest of the congregation.

Whether my church has one hundred or one thousand, I cannot focus on them all. I want to build disciples, so I spend intensive time with a fraction of the people to whom I minister. A few mouths get the biggest slices of my time-and-energy pie. And that opens me to charges of favoritism.

It's easy for others in the congregation to become jealous of the few who associate most closely with me. I am their pastor, too, they rightly reason, yet I spend less time with them. And they may have been here longer, and perhaps been even more committed to the church.

The pastor indeed carries pastoral responsibility for the entire fellowship. I accept the reality that everyone in the congregation must in some way sense my personal interest and support. I'm not free to neglect the preaching, administration, and other efforts for the "many" to minister to the "few."

But I'll be most effective by focusing on a few. Here are several tactics that allow me to do that while neutralizing the feeling that I'm playing favorites.

I do not make public statements about my few. I don't even say I have a few. That would be like saying, "I heard a great joke today, but I'm not telling you!" People will feel left out and resentful if I play up how wonderful my relationship is with a handful of trusted parishioners. I may not even identify to a person among the few that I am focusing on him or her. I don't need credit for offering a little more of myself to someone.

I do not focus on the few in a public setting. I define a *clique* as a group of people you can pick out in the midst of a bigger group because they clump together. So I use the motto, "Ministry in public, friendship in private." In a public setting, such as Sunday morning, the few and I disperse to minister to others. We know we will see each other at other times for personal interaction.

I give the whole congregation plenty of opportunity to be with me at a more personal level. I find numerous ways to say to the congregation, "Come be with me." People who want to get near me can do so in an evening Bible study, one-night seminars, and the occasional Sunday school class I teach. This invitation is offered to the whole congregation, and to members individually. I particularly welcome long-time members, the "old guard." They need to feel included in my ministry, too.

I minister to the many with the few. Of the thousands of people who crowded around Christ during his ministry, he concentrated on a mere twelve. But he sent *them* to minister. I love the comment of George Williams, founder of the YMCA in the last century: "We had only one thing in mind and that was to bind our little company together in order that we might better lead our comrades to Christ."

Not too long ago a man asked me, "Stan, I want to grow in my spiritual life. Would you meet with me?"

I said, "It would be a privilege to grow in Christ together. When I visit the hospitals on Friday afternoon, would you join me?" He agreed. For months we saw God at work in difficult situations in the hospital. After our visits, we would talk and pray together. Later this man went on to do some visitation by himself, and now he helps coordinate some aspects of our visitation. What began as ministry to one person has developed into ministry, through him, to many.

TEN

KEEPING VISITORS COMING BACK

Every person needs security. Every person needs to belong. Every person needs to believe that he or she has influence. Everybody needs self-esteem. When a church lives up to the potential God has given it, no organization does these things better.

HERB MILLER

What do you do if you discover your Sunday school is actually repelling instead of attracting visitors? Don Michael McDonald, teacher of an adult class in the Community Bible Church of San Bernardino, California, had a comfortable, informative class just like thousands of others, but that's the question he had to face. Knowing people join niches and not just churches, he was determined to find out what was wrong and how to make his niche attractive to newcomers.

As a result of what McDonald learned and put into practice, the class began to grow about 10 percent each month, and by the end of a year it had reached an average attendance of sixty-five. Perhaps the best indicator the new strategy was working was that 80 percent of class visitors returned. Here McDonald explains what he learned and how he made the turnaround.

David and Beverly stood in the doorway of the adult Sunday school class and looked over a sea of unfamiliar faces. Beverly had coaxed for weeks to get David there. Their first child was due in four months, and Beverly wanted that child to have a church home. David kept citing a bad experience with "religious people," but he was finally willing to try church again since they had just moved to this area.

Maybe this time I'll meet some nice people, David thought.

Maybe this time, Beverly prayed, *someone in there will introduce David to Jesus.*

I shudder to think how many Davids and Beverlys visited our class and walked away with needs unmet. We didn't realize it, but we weren't giving them a chance.

Our pastor first noticed the problem. He called one evening and asked if I would join him for breakfast at a local restaurant. "Sure," I said. "What's up?"

"We need to talk about the couples class."

I wasn't sure what he was driving at. Our class was well established; it had existed for fifteen of our church's thirty-five years, and I had taught or cotaught the group for eight years.

If anything, we were typical. I took up the offering and taught a Bible lesson. My wife, Judy, did everything else.

As we met that morning, the pastor pointed out that slowly, almost imperceptibly, our class was losing attendance. In a year's time our average attendance had dropped from twenty-five to twenty.

"Growth occurs on the edges," he said, "and you're not taking in new people." I didn't have any answers, but then, neither did the pastor. In the following months, however, as we prayed about and pondered the situation, we came to several conclusions.

Know Thy Purpose

We had begun a guest book several months earlier. As Judy and I examined it, we realized many people had visited, but we didn't recognize any of the names. None had ever returned! As a matter of fact, we couldn't think of any regular attenders who had been coming less than three years.

Why not? I worked hard on those Bible lessons. Our group seemed to enjoy studying God's Word and praying together.

We thought about what makes visitors come and realized it is usually because they have tried the worship hour, liked it, and are looking for deeper involvement. Bible study happens many places, but accepting new members begins in Sunday school.

Judy and I set a goal: have one visitor feel accepted and return. We defined acceptance as never having to feel or say, "I'm an outsider." With this in mind, we began to see contradictions between what we wanted and what we did.

Intimate or Accepting?

The class cannot be intimate and accepting at the same time, we found.

Our format felt comfortable. People entered and sat in a semicircle. We took an offering and asked for announcements, typically someone's illness and the need for a few meals to be brought over. Someone else often told of a recent answer to prayer. This led into conversational prayer and thanksgiving. Next, we turned to our Bible lesson, continued from the previous week. We closed with prayer.

Our regular attenders enjoyed the format and grew spiritually with it. But if we wanted to accept newcomers, something had to change. Our pastor asked one man why he and his wife didn't attend our class. The man shook his head. "I can't go in there again. They pray out loud. I can't do that." That man didn't feel comfortable praying by himself, much less eavesdropping on the prayers of people he didn't know.

Intimacy among old-timers is desirable, but the visitor calls it a clique. We decided to sacrifice intimacy if it prevented an accepting atmosphere. We knew scolding the regular attenders would not help. So we began to experiment with the class format.

We arranged the chairs in small circles and noticed an immediate change in attendance. We leaped from an average of twenty to twelve. If David and Beverly had walked through the door then, they would have been afraid to sit anywhere. If they began a circle, they would have had to sweat it out waiting for someone else, a stranger, to sit by them. On the other hand, if others were already seated, David and Beverly would fear taking the seats next to someone waiting for an old friend. We returned to the "one big arch" arrangement but with something learned. There are levels of fellowship, and I was asking the people for too much commitment too soon.

Acceptance One Step at a Time

Acceptance comes when the class offers natural steps to involvement. We created a progression, repeating it each week in case other newcomers dropped in.

1. We began with no one seated. A person walking in would see people standing and sipping coffee or tea, talking from behind the protective shield of a Styrofoam cup. At the

call to order, everyone chose seats (from multiple rows) at the same time.

2. We required no previous experience with the group. Prearranged announcements covered only upcoming events and programs. The lesson began with humor but not inside jokes; locking a visitor out of the punch line is fatal to growth.

We found singing worked poorly with fewer than thirty, because each person perceived his or her voice as too conspicuous. When we did sing, we kept songs simple and made words available, often displaying them up front so newcomers weren't the only ones looking at the words.

The lessons did not require knowledge from the previous week. For serial topics, we began each lesson by summarizing salient points from the previous lessons.

3. We required no previous experience with the Bible. The text was stated at the beginning of the lesson. Once people realized they needed Bibles, we offered them to everyone who did not have them, with the day's key verse already marked.

For those who had brought Bibles, we briefly explained how to find the key verse. The first time I explained that Psalms was in the middle of the Bible, one of our regulars laughed. But now our old-timers realize the person next to them truly may not know.

We geared questions to opinion, personal experience, or what could be answered solely from the morning's text.

4. We prepared people for greater participation. I asked people to form small circles only after they had milled around, chosen seats, and heard some content. And first I would instruct each person to be prepared to give first and last names and to answer a simple question about himself or herself. By having a few seconds to prepare their comments, people were not as apprehensive about starting conversations.

We had people jot their thoughts before we asked them to talk with the five or six people they'd just met. Only then did we ask for volunteers to answer the question before everyone.

As a result, timid people began speaking up more. Sometimes we'd hear, "Mark had a good answer. Go ahead, Mark. Tell him what you told us."

5. We discouraged natural group selection. We formed circles by various methods — parts of town the attenders were from, or birthdays. This kept old friends from clustering at the expense of newcomers.

In addition, we offered other avenues for meeting needs of deeper intimacy and Bible study. Regular attenders were encouraged to participate in supplemental Bible studies. We handled intimate prayer requests through auxiliary prayer chains. We invited people to join groups of four couples that would get together once a month for three months. After a while, 50 percent of the regular attenders were participating continuously.

We encouraged regulars to develop a ministry mentality. Once every five or six weeks we discussed how to help newcomers: What help do people need when new in town? What would make a newcomer comfortable in a crowd of strangers? Why do we structure the class this way? A new couple that Sunday would catch us talking about them, but the subject was how much we wanted them. Over the door of the classroom we placed the following acrostic: TTDCTFLOOC. It stands for "Through this door come the future leaders of our church." Regulars know they can no longer assume the person in the next chair is even a believer.

Our Class Grew

The class may have thought it was just another Sunday the first week a visitor returned, but Judy and I saw it as God's answer to our prayer. During the following months, we had to bring in more chairs. Our average weekly attendance began to climb about 10 percent each month. Within five months, attendance averaged about thirty. When one year had passed, we were sharing God's Word with sixty or seventy each week. During that year, 80 percent of class visitors returned. Some didn't return, of course, and some regular attenders left, but for every attender lost we gained four.

If growth had been in numbers only, we could claim no real gain. But our regular attenders began looking for opportunities to reach out to others and take an interest in their spiritual needs. Remember the man who said he couldn't pray aloud? He attends now, and recently he told Judy and me how he led his son in prayer for salvation.

Some might object, "But people don't like changes in our church." Remember, our class was in a rut worn fifteen years deep. Even established classes can change.

Others might object, "But we have no visitors." We were fortunate to have occasional drop-ins. One person told me that until recently he had never been motivated to bring friends. "Why expose them to a situation you know they won't like?" An accepting atmosphere helps people risk bringing a friend.

As the class has grown, more people have become involved by necessity. That, too, makes the class more meaningful to them. Before the change, Judy and I got tired of doing everything. Now, about 30 percent of the attenders help by bringing refreshments or leading outside Bible studies. People volunteer when they see their efforts will count. We first had to demonstrate that something was happening, that our class had a purpose. We've focused ours on acceptance.

"You know," said David as he and Beverly left the class after visiting a while ago, "that guy who sat next to me has the same carburetor problem with his car. I want to talk to him next week."

E L E V E N

"PASTOR, I'M LEAVING"

All sorrow and suffering are designed to teach us lessons we would not or could not learn in any other way.

MAX HEINDEL

Three of the most painful words pastors ever hear are "Pastor, I'm leaving." The message they convey is the opposite of what we want to hear. The temptation to take the news personally is almost irresistible. We wonder, What did I do or fail to do that's causing them to leave? *And then comes the agonizing question,* How could they do this to me? *The hurt and self-doubt never get easier, even though the situation is inevitable.*

John Cionca, dean of students at Bethel Seminary and former pastor of Southwood Baptist Church in Woodbury, New Jersey, asked fellow pastors how they have handled the pain of losing members and what lessons they have learned from the experience about making something good come out of it. He tells what has helped, and he also suggests how best to handle the situation so as to maximize the possibility that those leaving may someday return.

When Jack, a fellow pastor and friend, arrived for dinner, I could see he was troubled. Later he revealed the source of his dejection: "Today one of my key leaders told me he's leaving the church." The member wasn't moving out of town. Just leaving.

While Jack spoke, I felt my own anger and hurt resurfacing from similar experiences in the pastorate. I wanted to help him, but other than sharing his discouragement over the loss of disgruntled members, how could I?

I decided to ask a dozen colleagues how they handle the emotional fallout from dropout members.

A Common Denominator

All of them share a sense of failure when a family leaves the church. A pastor in the Southwest admitted: "Sometimes I have been able to say, 'Well, you can't win them all.' But when I'm alone with my thoughts, my mind wanders back to those people. I try to guess what's behind their leaving. I know I can't minister to everybody, but it hurts when people leave." Another observed: "No matter how much explanation people give to assure me that 'It's not you, Pastor,' I still feel that pain personally." Pastors typically accept overall responsibility for the church's ministry. Whether the unhappiness is with an adult class, the youth ministry, or the music, the minister always feels the sting.

"You can usually narrow the reasons for leaving to a few,"one pastor told me. "People feel they don't belong, they don't agree with some doctrine, they want a different style of program, or they don't have any friends. Often they say they're 'not being fed.' "

But since the church often reflects the pastor's personality and philosophy of ministry, when a member announces, "I'm leaving the church," pastors translate that, "I'm rejecting you!"

Contributors to the Pain

A number of factors affect how deeply a pastor will feel the loss:

The Personality Factor. On psychological inventories such as the Taylor-Johnson Temperament Analysis or the MMPI, pastors' scores vary on scales regarding sensitivity versus indifference, subjectivity versus objectivity, or relational orientation versus task orientation. But our profession necessitates building relationships, and therefore most ministers are in a position to be hurt by people who seemingly reject their ministry. The more sensitive, subjective, or relational one's personality, the more intense will be the hurt.

The Surprise Factor. Often we're not surprised by someone's leaving. Some members let their disagreement be known, and we are psychologically prepared for their departure. But when a couple just disappears and we hear rumors they're attending elsewhere, we take that news much harder.

The surprise factor definitely had an impact on my friend Jack. Fred, who left his church, taught an adult Sunday school class. He was preparing to coordinate the home Bible study program. The previous Sunday, Fred had assisted Jack in the chancel. Then Monday morning he told Jack that he and his family were leaving the church. The greater the surprise, the more likely the wind will be knocked out of us.

The Investment Factor. Pastor Ron poured a lot of time and energy into the Johnsons, and Joan Johnson grew in her church responsibilities. Then she began to struggle in her marriage. For eighteen months the church cared for the Johnsons, supporting their marriage, watching their children, praying for them. In the end, however, Joan decided she wanted out of her family — and out of the church.

Ron's personal theology of ministry was at risk with the Johnsons. The couple's active involvement affirmed his philosophy of ministry that all people should have the opportunity to use their gifts in the local church. "When I saw her blossom, I felt she justified my philosophy," Ron recalls. "I had a lot of chips on the table, and when she left, I felt like I lost them. It challenged my theology." The more we have invested in a member, the more it hurts when one leaves.

The Statistical Factor. Departing members damage statistics, and whether we like it or not, we are influenced by the statistical assumption, at least emotionally, that a successful pastor is one whose church is growing. A pastor who has "built" his church is more attractive than the pastor of a dwindling congregation.

No one knows this better than a small-church pastor. When Westinghouse transferred one family to New York, a church I was in lost 3 percent of its Sunday school.

The second part of the statistical factor is income. A church that is meeting or exceeding its budget appears more successful than a church struggling with finances. When a tithing family leaves, their loss is felt financially. In a small church, that tithe may be a substantial percentage of the budget, and the decrease in statistics may cause some to question the pastor's leadership.

The Prestige Factor. During my last pastorate, one particular loss hurt me deeply because of the couple's prestige. Ben and Alice were long-time church members. For over a decade, Ben had served as a deacon and worship leader. He was chairman of the search committee that called me.

Sixteen months into my ministry, Ben said that he and Alice would be leaving the church. Gracious people, they didn't make any waves. I highly respected them and understood their reasons. But Ben was a pillar of the church, a nationally known evangelical leader, and a board member of my seminary.

While we tell ourselves we can't scratch where everyone itches, we sure would like to scratch effectively for people like Ben and Alice. Losing them affects us significantly.

The Spin-off Factor. I am convinced the most important ingredient for church growth is congregational attitude and esteem. When someone leaves the church to attend a different one, it's a blow to a church's self-esteem. When more than one family leaves, people begin to wonder, *What's going on around here? What's wrong with us?*

Because they know someone's leaving hurts the church's self-esteem, pastors feel the loss doubly.

Coping with the Inevitable

Some sheep will inevitably move elsewhere, so how can pastors cope with the feelings of hurt, loss, and failure that accompany these migrations? As I mulled over the responses from my colleagues, I arrived at several conclusions:

Concede that people will leave your ministry. You've heard the expression, "What you don't know can't hurt you." Not so! Mid-life men need to anticipate career restlessness, and older couples should count on the empty-nest syndrome. So must pastors anticipate the reality of losing members through discontent.

One pastor put it: "I try to take heart by remembering that it has happened before and it will happen again. People will leave, but it's not the end of the world. Every pastor in the country has faced it."

Praise God for diversity. People are different. That's why

McDonald's, Taco Bell, and Kentucky Fried Chicken all stay in business. People don't leave their preferences at home when they attend church. They appreciate different styles of worship, program, and involvement. One pastor considered such preferences not necessarily bad: "Just as some pastors would not appeal to me if I were sitting in the pew, I recognize I will not appeal to everyone, either."

Another minister noted, "There are differences in gifts and styles of ministry, and at the present, some individual may need something else."

The Lord is building his universal church, and a subtraction from my particular congregation might actually be a blessing. One pastor wisely observed: "There are some people the Lord might move on. Maybe down the road you'll see that by his grace he protected you from deeper problems. Sometimes it's best for you and the overall welfare of the church when people leave."

Look beyond the complaint to the concern. In one church, I was asked to resolve a dispute over having a woman teach an adult Sunday school class. This woman had taught previously in the adult elective program, but for two years she had been sidelined until the elders could "study the issue." After two marathon sessions, the board concluded she could teach.

Although the board strongly endorsed the decision, one elder who held a very conservative view resigned. To my surprise, the woman and her husband also left the church shortly thereafter.

The dispute over teaching was only a surface issue. What the woman really wanted was for me to say, "Yes, I understand that you have been hurt and not treated fairly." She primarily sought love and affirmation of her worth. Only secondarily did she desire resolution of the teaching issue.

I had rolled up my sleeves and attacked the surface problem but had failed to communicate my concern for her personally. I wish I had heard then the advice given by one pastor: "I try to get beyond my feelings to focus on the hurts of the person leaving."

Accept criticism where applicable. Even after people quit, we can't simply write them off. One pastor said, "After people leave, I feel guilty: Have I tried everything? Was I fair? Was I open enough?" People's absence leaves us with nagging questions.

Another minister stated: "Maybe I've done something wrong. Maybe something is lacking either in my personal ministry or the ministry of the church. So I try to honestly evaluate what is said to see if there is truth in it." While we might not retain disgruntled members, their loss may point out personal shortcomings that, when corrected, will help us with other people in the future.

Process your feelings with another person. One of the questions I asked my friends was, "How do you get back on track after a family has left?" There was great overlap on one response: "Talk it out with a friend."

"I try to share my burden with another pastor who understands," one advised. "People who aren't in the ministry often don't comprehend what it feels like when someone leaves, so I meet with pastors who have experienced and understand the same circumstances."

A pastor of a larger church noted that he confided in the staff members. "We compare notes. Maybe I don't know the whole story. Though the rejection is still there, it gets easier if you can discuss it."

Another pastor confides in a key layman: "I feel comfortable sharing with him. He may not have the answer, but just being able to talk with him helps." Whether we talk with a spouse, a board member, a staff member, or a pastor friend, a loving listener seems to aid in healing the hurt experienced when someone leaves.

Leaving the Door Open

Knowing people are unhappy with my ministry is disquieting; going to them when they're leaving is utterly disconcerting. Nevertheless, some pastors contact people who leave the church.

Ken Trivilla at Wooddale Church in Eden Prairie, Minnesota, conducts an exit interview, believing the information gained will benefit the church. The Wooddale staff feels everyone who leaves the church should be given a "proper burial." Ken says, "I want to leave people with the feeling they can return if they want to. I always try to meet people personally, face to face."

What's sometimes hard is interviewing people you're glad are leaving. "One man left because he felt he was able to teach better than some of our teachers," Ken recalls. "I took him to lunch and listened to his grievances. When it became apparent I was not trying to woo him back to the church but was just allowing him to share his concerns, he got angry."

In another situation, Wooddale had put a couple to work too quickly. Ken says, "They had come from a church in Chicago, and in the fall we put them in a teaching slot. By December they decided to leave our church. I called them right away and tried to rebuild our bridges. They didn't return, but we parted good friends."

Whatever the technique used, I want the particulars of a given situation to determine my response. A couple of times I have met with the people to talk about their leaving. I have also phoned members who had begun attending another church. In two other situations I wrote people a cordial letter indicating I recognized their departure and wished the best for them.

In each of the circumstances I felt it was important to do three things: First, I wanted to apologize if either my demeanor or our church ministry offended them. If there were any barrier on my part, I wanted it removed. Who was at fault was not the issue.

Second, I wanted to reaffirm our philosophy of church ministry. I did not want them to think our church's direction would necessarily change simply because they were unhappy with it.

Third, I wanted to leave the door wide open for their return. If they subsequently learned the pews were not softer on the other side of the block, I hoped they would feel free to return. I remained on cordial terms with all six families that left our church, and one eventually came back into our fellowship.

Researching this article has encouraged me. Not that the reality of my friends' pain was encouraging, but I was uplifted by the fact we were a fellowship of ministers experiencing the same concerns and affirming one another.

We can learn from our injuries and grow through our pain. And we may become God's messengers to other colleagues when they, too, hear the words: "Pastor, I'm leaving."

TWELVE

MINISTRY TO MISSING MEMBERS

I wonder if anyone ever misses the missing?

LYLE SCHALLER

The perception church leaders have of inactive members is linked to the actions they intend to take about inactivity.

MARK S. JONES

Simply talking to inactive members is difficult. Asking them why they dropped out is like opening the spigot on a water tower full of grievances both real and imagined. John Savage leads us into this troubled area and says we've got our work cut out for us in drawing these people back into active fellowship. But he doesn't leave us there. He shows us how to understand the missing and how to meet their needs.

Not surprisingly, this chapter was one of the highest-rated articles in LEADERSHIP's history. Savage, president of L.E.A.D. Consultants in Reynoldsburg, Ohio, studied the problem for more than ten years and interviewed inactive members from four churches. Here he explains what he learned about why people choose to become inactive and what can be done to bring them back to full participation.

I was going through slides I had used in an every-member canvass in my church. When I held some to the window, I was shocked. Pictured in the first three slides were three couples who had held key offices in the church my first year there. Now, four years later, those couples were totally inactive.

These people no longer attended worship, except maybe on Christmas or Easter, made no financial contribution, didn't participate in the life of the church, and had a negative attitude about the congregation.

How could people move in just four years from active involvement to total inactivity? I wondered.

I thought of times I had visited inactive members and seen absolutely nothing happen. In fact, often they were more convinced to stay away *after* I made the call. I knew I needed to figure out how to keep current members active and enable inactive ones to return.

Anxiety-provoking Events

I went to work on these questions as I pursued a doctorate and have continued to search for answers over the last decade.

I tried to find studies about the phenomenon, but I dug up nothing. So, with a psychologist and a theologian, I designed a research project. Thirteen trained pastors and I interviewed inactive members from four United Methodist congregations to find out what caused them to disappear from church life.

We found 95 percent of the people had experienced what we now call an "anxiety-provoking event" — an APE. Subsequent research showed these events usually come in clusters, several APEs compounding within six months to a year.

Anxiety is the emotional alarm system that is triggered when we're in disequilibrium, when we've been hurt or feel that unless a change is made we're going to get hurt. The inactive members we visited revealed high levels of anxiety, which when unresolved drove them from church membership. Gradually we saw their anxiety fell into four categories.

Reality anxiety. This anxiety is based on some real, historical event; you could have videotaped what caused it. Normally the event is a snub or an utter lack of church care when a member most needed it.

Suppose a pastor preaches his first sermon at a new church and someone says, "Pastor, we've had some lousy preachers here, but I think you're going to be the worst." That's an anxiety-provoking event for a pastor, and it's reality anxiety.

A while back I preached in a church in Vancouver. Two days prior, a family from the church had their home burn to the ground, and their 2- and 4-year-old children died in the fire. The father, in an attempt to save his youngest, dashed into the bedroom. The walls and curtains were on fire, as were the bedding and the child's clothing. Leaning over to snatch the child out of the fire, severely burning himself in the process, the father tried to pick up his child. The child's body fell apart in his hands.

How many people went to visit him and his wife? Maybe the pastor, but probably not many parishioners. Most would confess, "I wouldn't know what to say," as if they had to say something. A family experiencing the horror of this kind of tragedy would have a hard time returning to a church they felt let them down when they needed them. That is a reality anxiety-provoking event.

Moral anxiety. This next type is more difficult because it isn't always as obvious. Moral anxiety arises when people experience in themselves or others behaviors they believe aren't right.

A lay person called me once and said, "I understand you work with churches where people are leaving."

"That's true."

"Well," he continued, "our senior pastor has admitted having an affair with a woman in the congregation, our associate pastor confessed a homosexual affair with our organist, and we have four choir members involved in affairs."

That large church has lost more members over moral anxiety than most churches will ever have.

Moral anxiety can also be private yet still drive people from the church. In *Meetings at the Edge,* Steven Levine tells the story of a devout Christian nurse who cared for Evie, a woman who was given permission by her family to end her life because of the extreme pain caused by cancer. Helen, the nurse, refused to participate in such an act. Yet Evie persisted. She planned to take the barbiturate-laced applesauce at 9 P.M. Helen reluctantly agreed to arrive at 10 and do whatever she could if Evie were not yet dead.

As Helen entered the house, Evie was crying. She was frightened and could not take the applesauce alone. She asked Helen to feed it to her. Helen said, "I cannot," and walked out to sit in her car.

Ten minutes later, Evie hobbled to the door using a chair like a walker. She was vomiting. "Please come help me!" she begged. "I don't want to be trapped in a coma and only partially die. Please come!" Helen walked into the house, fed her the rest of the applesauce, and held Evie until she died.

There's a good chance Helen was not in church the following Sunday, and no one would know why. Her moral anxiety-provoking event was private.

Neurotic anxiety. The types get more difficult to handle as we go down the list. Neurotic anxiety is pain caused by the imagination. Someone may claim, "I don't go to church because the pastor doesn't like me." If you check it out, the feeling might be based on reality, but the chances are it's neurotic. It's only in the person's head.

A man goes into the hospital, expects you to visit, but doesn't let you know he's there. Then he gets angry when you don't call. Months later when you do call, you may trace his problem to that hospital stay. The man is convinced you don't care about him. That's neurotic anxiety.

Even more frustrating than the fact that the person's grievance is imaginary is that we can inadvertently foster it. For example, a pastor regularly calls on a couple who are potential members. He spends time with them and makes them feel important. All the time they're thinking, *Look at all the personal attention you get from the pastor around here!* Then they join the church, and the attention they receive drops almost to zero. They wonder what happened. The pastor has accidentally encouraged unrealistic expectations, which give rise to neurotic anxiety.

Existential anxiety. Existential anxiety is that feeling brought about by the thought that some day you may not exist, or that even if you do, your life may be meaningless. We hear the refrains, "The church has lost its meaning for me," "The sermons don't mean anything anymore, Pastor," "My kids are bored stiff in church school."

I visited a family that had been active church members but had dropped out. As I talked with them, I learned that when they were preparing for marriage, the pastor said to the bride, "I believe you're a born-again Christian, but I'm not convinced your fiancé is. If you marry him, your first child will die." I was talking with them six months after their 3-year-old boy had died.

They experienced existential anxiety at its height. Twenty minutes into that conversation, the couple cried as hard as two adults could cry. Tears running down the cheek begin to say something of the nature of the pain encountered when visiting an inactive member.

Clusters of Events

Most often people who drop out have run into these four types of anxiety in clusters. For example, a man in my congregation lost his job, and the family income plummeted to nothing. His wife, under stress, ended up depressed and in a mental hospital for two weeks. Soon after, this couple — active leaders in our church — were told they were doing an inadequate job as youth leaders and then were abruptly dismissed. They became angry and quit coming to church.

When a lay person and I visited them some weeks later, the woman was reading a newspaper. She put it down, said hello, and put it right back up. That's called resistance. We talked with her husband, and in about five minutes she slammed the paper into her lap. We had before us a red-faced, angry woman.

The first thing inactive people mention is usually the last event in the anxiety-provoking cluster. "We're just as good youth leaders as anybody else up at that church!" she informed us. "If we aren't good enough for that, we aren't good enough for anything."

It's easy to assume that's the sole or primary issue, but it's not. The unresolved anxiety of the *cluster* of events has made this final event intolerable. Until we uncover and deal with the original pain of the cluster, even if it happened twenty years ago, people will likely remain outside the church.

We talked for some time with these people. I'm happy to report they did come back to church and eventually accepted new leadership responsibilities.

Arenas of Conflict

Anxiety — of whatever variety — arises from some problem. The most common is *intrafamily conflict.* Husband and wife square off on some issue; parents and kids squabble. This kind of conflict is the most consistent characteristic of people who have left the church.

Conflict with pastors is the second most common problem,

and the main cause is avoidance. When pastors avoid dealing with people's anxiety, the people simply avoid the pastors and their churches.

Family against family, *interfamily conflict*, is the third arena. It's the Hatfields against the McCoys; people don't get along with one another.

Overwork, or at least the feeling of it, presents a fourth problem area. With volunteer church service, too much too soon or too long, with no reward, will drive people from the church.

Suppose you discover a family whose members are having troubles at home, seem to be avoiding you, are feeling disappointed about the way other church members have treated them, and think they're overworked and unrewarded. You will usually find they are experiencing reality, moral, neurotic, or existential anxiety — often simultaneously. Then you can predict the next stage: they cry for help.

The Cry for Help

If we learn to hear and respond to people's cries for help, we can usually prevent their dropping out, because most of those still crying for help will respond to our efforts to reach them. But cries don't last forever. Some cry longer than others, depending on their bond to the congregation, but when the cry goes unanswered, eventually members leave. Then the damage is much greater and more difficult to repair.

So how does a cry for help sound? It comes in all forms, sizes, and intensities. A verbal cry for help may sound like this: "I don't know if I want to continue coming to this church. If there is one thing I can't stand, it's hypocrites!" Or it could be more subtle, like the one I heard years back: "You know, all the men but me in our Sunday school class have had promotions at work."

I worked with a woman in Christian education for two years and never once heard any complaint. Then one day, in the midst of a long paragraph, she let slip just one sentence:

"I'm not sure I can do this job much longer." Those words stuck out to me as if PROBLEM were bracketed in my head.

I didn't say anything right then, but when I saw her the next Sunday morning in the hallway, I said, "Sally, I have a feeling you might be upset about some things in church, particularly in C.E."

She put her head on my shoulder and said, "John, can I talk with you this week?"

She came in the following Thursday with all her teaching materials — unmistakable body language. Even before she sat down, she said, "You're not going to like what I'm about to tell you, but I'm going to resign." I listened to her story for an hour and a half, and I heard from her the classical phraseology of one who is thinking of leaving: "I don't want to leave the church. I love the church, but I'm tired." She was over-worked — reality anxiety — so we renegotiated her work-load, and she stayed. The key is hearing the story first.

The cries for help are more numerous than we realize. At one large church, I asked people to listen at church for cries for help. Thirty-three people listened one Sunday morning. The fewest cries anyone heard was two. I heard twelve. The group was shocked by the scores of cries we tallied.

Three Responses

Pastors can respond to cries in one of three ways.

First, they can listen and respond to the pain the cry represents, and that can be amazingly beneficial.

Second, they can ignore the cry, not realizing how serious it is, until the cry moves into anger. The person gets more agitated and says, in effect, "Hey, what do I have to do around here to get you to hear me? Somebody help me! Can't you see I'm about to leave the church?"

Third, they can shoot the person with the gospel gun: "Hey, Buddy, what's the matter with you? You losing your faith or something?" That's a mistake of confusing the symptom for the disease, the behavior for the cause. But surprisingly, even if we react to the immediate anger rather than the anxiety behind it, we'll still recover about 80 percent of the people. Even hesitating steps in the right direction can help.

If we miss the verbal cries for help, we at least have a whole string of nonverbal cries to alert us to the problem. The cries for help become behavioral. The person either leaves or begins the process of leaving.

The first behavior change is the leaving of worship. Second, people leave major committees and boards. They either don't show up or they begin to show up sporadically. Both of these indicators can be seen on an attendance graph. The one who was always there four Sundays a month drops to three to two to only rare appearances. Or the board member makes one or two meetings a year after nearly perfect attendance in past years.

Third, people begin to leave Sunday school. This may vary from denomination to denomination, but most adults have their closest friends in their Sunday school classes. Backing away from friends is a major change.

Fourth, the kids are pulled out of Sunday school. The parents decide they don't even want to bring them, let alone come themselves.

Fifth comes the letter of resignation, and finally, interestingly enough, the pledge is dropped. That's the final gasp for help, the last commitment to be given up in most denominations.

The sad thing is, these dropouts are hurting. They've experienced not only a private cluster of anxiety-provoking events, but now they're also grieving the loss of the church from their lives.

Skunks and Turtles

In my original research, a full third of the inactive people we called on had tears running down their cheeks once we dug out the original cluster of pain. Uncovering that hurt caused them to cry before perfect strangers.

These people need desperately to be heard, and when they aren't, *helplessness* sets in. They begin to blame something *external* — the church, the pastor. We've nicknamed them *skunks*. When you call on these people, you get sprayed on. It's what happened to me when the woman slammed the paper into her lap and lashed out at me.

When these people drop out, they wait six to eight weeks and then psychologically seal off the pain and anxiety produced by the original cluster. They back away and by all appearances become apathetic. But the pain of that cluster remains in the unconscious and acts as the block to returning to church. In order to get the person to come back, we must deal with that pain. Otherwise we'll hear every excuse under the sun for not returning.

After they seal off the pain, people reinvest their time, energy, and money in other pursuits. Half reinvest themselves in the family; they buy tents, trailers, and snowmobiles and go away on the weekend. You visit them and you hear, "Now our family is just as close to God up fishing on the lake as we were back at church with that bunch of snobs." This family still consider themselves Christians. Guess who they consider not the Christian? If we go to them in an attempt to "save" them, we're in for the scrap of our lives, because they consider themselves more Christian than us.

The other 50 percent reinvest themselves in other institutions: hospitals, PTA, Girl Scouts, Boy Scouts, Rotary. So if we call on them, they'll point their fingers at us and say, "I've gotten involved with that volunteer ambulance crew. I'm a dispatcher on Sunday mornings. You know, we *really* help people now." That's a skunk speaking.

Another set of dropouts experiences a different emotion: *hopelessness.* It's the antithesis of helplessness. It's the sense of being incapable of generating any inner motivation. As a result, these people withdraw and become inactive. We call them *turtles.*

Turtles have incredible power to hook other people's guilt. A turtle's cry for help might sound like this: "I'm sure you could get Mrs. Green to teach the class. She would do a much better job than I could." The turtle drops out, waits six to eight weeks, and seals off the pain, much like the skunk. But turtles point the blame internally, toward themselves.

Whether it's the skunks' spray or the turtles' timidity, the various cries for help can be addressed.

Responding to Cries for Help

So what do we do for these people? We need to teach ourselves and our lay people to hear the pain of inactive people. It helps, too, if we learn how to intervene in the stages leading up to inactivity, before the people disappear from sight in a whirl of emotion.

One way we did this in a church I served was to take fifteen minutes at the end of every board meeting for the board members to report who, in their estimation, was crying for help. We collected those names and gave them to a team of twenty-four trained callers. Pastors can never do all the calling, so as a pastor I aimed for a corps of up to 10 percent of the congregation that I prepared to visit the inactives.

I also extended my secretary's hours so she could stand near me at the door on Sunday mornings to listen for cries for help. She was good at picking them up, and I could inconspicuously indicate others for her to note while I managed the flurry of smiles and handshakes and small talk. By the afternoon, she would alert the calling teams, who would reach out to these people *before* their cries turned to the silence of absence. Prior to that, I'd often hear several cries on a Sunday morning but fail to remember them or follow up on them.

When we call on an inactive family, or one heading that direction, the chances are strong we're going to have to deal with anger. The turtles' anger will make us feel guilty, and the skunks' anger will make us mad. Since calling on an inactive member is often painful, it's easy to enter a cycle: People leave because they're angry; I'm angry because they left; I punish them by letting them sit in their pain; they punish me by not coming back.

That's where reconciliation must enter. Active members of the church go to an inactive member on behalf of the community in an act of reconciliation. If we are willing to bear some pain with the inactive person, reconciliation will often occur.

Look at what God did. We wouldn't listen to him, so he made a pastoral call to his inactive members. He sent his own Son, who called on us and suffered on the cross for us. That kind of self-giving love got our attention and enabled us to be reconciled to him.

We will not get inactive members back by avoiding pain. We have to take the initiative, go to them, uncover the anxiety-provoking cluster, hear and often bear their pain, and thus pave the road for them to return.

Ultimately, we have to remember we call not to get people to come back to church. We call because people are in pain. If they come back as a result of our ministering to their pain, that is good. But if they don't, we have still reached out to them in the name of Jesus Christ.

THIRTEEN

HOW TO KEEP LAY WORKERS FROM BURNING OUT

Burnout victims start out full of fire and good intentions, but their efforts are not repaid in kind. The reality is that it is difficult to help people.

PAUL CHANCE

And let us not grow weary while doing good, for in due season we shall reap if we do not lose heart.

GALATIANS 6:9

Faithful lay workers — the unsung heroes of every church, the people whose active participation makes ministry possible. We motivate them to reach out, to meet the needs of others, but sometimes these stalwarts run the risk of burnout. Our most reliable workers could be the next people out the back door if we neglect a few basic rules of lay ministry.

From her own volunteer experiences both good and bad, Virginia Vagt, a homemaker and active lay worker, describes the kind of ministry that led her to burnout and leaving one church, and the different kind of ministry in another church that proved fruitful and enjoyable and kept her excited over the long haul. The principles she learned from these vastly different experiences show how we can keep our unsung heroes enthusiastically active in the work of the local church.

I *don't want to go to church tomorrow,* I remember moaning to myself Saturday after Saturday during my final months at Resurrection Church. It wasn't the pastor, his sermons, or a lack of warmth in the congregation that caused me to dread driving up the church's gravel driveway every Sunday.

Being 26 years old and trying to find my place in church life, my problem was that I was in over my head in a program called Women's Outreach. The founder of this program, Margaret Schiller, did lay mission work in Honduras every summer with her dentist husband. Her lifelong commitment to outreach was exciting. When she asked me to be one of her workers, to make weekly visits to a poverty-stricken young widow, I eagerly said yes. The extrovert in me and my need to find a meaningful ministry seemed to have found a good match.

Margaret put me in touch with Lisa, who lived with her 2-year-old son in a nearby low-income apartment building. What exactly was I supposed to do in my visits with Lisa? Other than "befriend her," I didn't know, but I felt reassured; Margaret told me the Lord would lead me.

At first, the dreary apartment building with its dark halls didn't deter me. Lisa would open the thin, scuffed door each

Saturday and offer me her warm smile. For several weeks we just sat and talked the way new friends do. Lisa seemed grateful to see me, and I felt I was doing God's work.

As I drove back and forth, however, I questioned myself: *What* is *my purpose? Is Lisa's life supposed to turn around and improve because I visit her? Is Lisa supposed to become a Christian through my friendship? Should I convince her to come to church?* With no answers, I just waited to see what would happen.

As the weeks went by, Lisa came up with all sorts of things *she* wanted me to do. One was baby-sitting for Danny, her son, while she and her cousin went off for an hour — or most of the day! It was unsettling not knowing how long I'd be alone with Danny in that apartment. On other occasions, Lisa asked me to drive her places so she could shop and visit. I never knew how long we'd be gone or where exactly we'd be going.

On some Saturdays, five or six of Lisa's friends and cousins would come over. Men would sit together on the plastic-upholstered couch while the women talked and laughed and looked at me as I played with Danny. On those days I felt conspicuous, outnumbered, and filled with self-doubt.

In frustration I wanted to say, "I didn't come here to baby-sit for you, drive you places, or be a specimen for your friends to look at." Before the words could come out, however, I answered them myself: *Then why* did *you come here?* Since I didn't know, how was Lisa supposed to know?

On Sundays, in the church basement next to the coffee pot and Styrofoam cups, Margaret would ask me how my visits with Lisa were going. I wanted to have a good report, to be able to say I was being helpful to Lisa or "We're making progress."

I felt too guilty to say to Margaret, "I don't know what I'm doing. I'm afraid of being in Lisa's apartment building. And I wish I never had to go back." Instead I said, "Well, I don't really know what to say or do specifically, and I feel a little lost."

Margaret responded with suggestions. One was for me to

teach Lisa how to shop for values and not waste money on junk food. Theoretically, that was a good suggestion. Lisa did need to learn things like that. But I never felt comfortable suggesting to Lisa that I knew how to shop and she didn't.

Margaret also suggested that I do a Bible study with Lisa. A Bible study sounded good; that was the kind of thing I had imagined we'd do together. And yet, which one? How would I start? If I found a good one, would Lisa think I was turning the tables on her, setting my own agenda? The Bible study never happened.

At the two-month point, I felt panicky about visiting Lisa. Without any goals or guidelines, the program was always in her hands. I felt caught between the possibility of Lisa's rejecting me and Margaret's feeling I was "not a good Christian." I was also unhappy that my Saturdays were being eaten up by a rocky friendship in which I had no real sense that the Lord was leading me.

Looking back on it, there are many things I should have done differently. But it was early in my adulthood and early in my experience in church work. Back then, I thought that if someone was in need, God wanted me to "give till it hurt." While I still believe there's some truth to that, my problem wasn't giving too much or too little but not knowing what I was doing and not having any hope that the situation would improve.

So, one Saturday, after sixteen weeks of visits, I said good-by to Lisa, and powered by the twin engines of guilt and fear, I never went back to Resurrection Church — and never said good-by to Margaret, the pastor, or anyone else in the congregation. My guilt came from feeling I had failed. The fear was that Margaret would talk me into giving it another try.

The one thing I knew was that I wasn't going to visit Lisa anymore.

Immature of me? Yes. Cowardly? Yes. And I doubt the pastor at Resurrection Church ever knew or even guessed why I left.

Learning How to Do Church Work

After my flight from Resurrection and several years of church hopping, my new husband, Peter, and I landed at a little stone church called St. Mark's. We attended for ten straight weeks and received a warm pastoral visit followed by a phone call. Would we like to team teach the high school Sunday school class?

Peter was a high school teacher, so that was a good fit, but I had never taught any kind of class. In spite of my lack of experience, however, panic didn't set in. Teaching together sounded like a good idea.

The "good idea" stretched into a four-year success experience. In addition to teaching, we took the kids on retreats and spent time with them after church. Peter and I grew spiritually. By having to prepare material for them, we learned more Bible ourselves than we ever would have on our own. The high school kids even christened us "the sunshine family." It felt good to get that kind of affirmation from kids. We kept asking ourselves, "Why is this week-after-week, time-consuming commitment working so well?"

As I look back, these are some of the factors that made our teaching at St. Mark's work well, and that by their absence had made my involvement in Women's Outreach a failure.

Someone to learn from. At St. Mark's, I wasn't thrown into cold water without a life preserver. Peter already knew how to teach. He knew what he was doing and was there to help me week after week. I could *observe* him in action before I had to do the same thing myself.

Going slowly. That first Sunday morning when large and small teenagers began to walk into our classroom, I felt scared. But in those early days, Peter let me solo for just five minutes at a time. As the weeks went by, I took ten-minute segments, then fifteen, and so on until I was able to take half the class time.

Regular debriefing. Each week we'd go home and talk over how our teaching went. Skits didn't work, but drawing posters on the spot to generate discussion did. With our weekly postmortems, failures became something to learn from and laugh about together. Successes made us glow.

The buddy system. For Peter, an experienced teacher, working with a novice had additional rewards. He wasn't just given another group of kids to teach. Instead, he also gained the satisfaction of sharing what he knew about teaching. He saw someone else — me — start to succeed as a teacher as a result of his modeling.

A supervisor to help. When we both ran into problems, the Sunday school superintendent was available for consultation. Teaching Christian sexual ethics to teenagers on Sunday morning, for example, wasn't something we felt confident about. Our superintendent spent several evenings on the phone helping us plan our approach. She kept in touch when she knew we were struggling or trying something different.

Avoiding a rut and passing the baton. Forgive the mixed metaphor, but after four years, it seemed time for a break. We could tell we had lost our freshness with high schoolers. Both of us were being asked to take on other church responsibilities, too. So we asked if we could train other adults to take our place.

The idea was accepted. Before packing up our magic markers and discussion-starter games, we met with other adults who wanted to begin working with high schoolers. At the close of our teaching years, we both had the satisfaction of training others the way Peter had trained me.

A Lesson in Burnout Prevention

Eight years after leaving Women's Outreach, I began ministry visits to another woman. But this time, our visits worked. As with the above Sunday school teaching, the secret was in training and ongoing support. Without that, I might have thrown up my hands with Sarah, a tired 82-year-old caught in the crucible of old age.

The primary source of help to me in this instance was our local senior citizen center's "friendly visitor" program. The program gave me guidelines and people to call when I wasn't sure what to do, such as how to be helpful to Sarah during the week she moved from her duplex to a nursing home.

As a result of monthly volunteer meetings and the program guidelines, I've been able to maintain my commitment, listen and smile to a lonely person, and be a fresh face in the world of the elderly. This time, we do talk about God and Christ, and we pray for each other's needs. It just took time.

Perhaps there would be less burnout if more churches could adopt some of the training and support techniques that volunteer organizations often use and that Peter and I unconsciously discovered at St. Mark's. Here are some of the important principles I saw in action at the friendly visitor program:

Screening. Before becoming a friendly visitor, I was interviewed. The director wanted to know *why* I wanted to minister in this way. Apparently most volunteers do want to help people, but they also need to feel the work is satisfying to them. If they don't, they'll quit.

My motives were wanting to improve my listening and empathic skills. Also, being without extended family in this state, I wanted a relationship with an older person. I saw it, too, as part of my Christian responsibility to visit those in need. The director thought my reasons were a good match to the purpose of the program, and I was accepted.

After that interview, I thought, *No one at church has ever asked me why I want to teach or be on the Stewardship Commission.* Perhaps if screening questions were asked at church, more people would end up in the right jobs and would last longer in those positions. At the very least, it would help clarify what we want and what we'll need to do the task.

Purpose. It sounds so simple, but how often in church do we nail down our purpose? The friendly visitor director told us our purpose was not to do grocery shopping or to clean the kitchen for our seniors. Our purpose, rather, was to listen and be a bright spot in their week. There were other community services such as Meals on Wheels and Dial-a-Ride to provide daily necessities. If we spent our time cleaning kitchens, how could we be good listeners and empathizers?

In the high school ministry at church, we realized our purpose was not to become "overgrown high schoolers" ourselves, but to be adult role models for them, to help guide them in their spiritual and social growth.

Signing on the dotted line. All friendly visitors have to sign an ethical statement and promise to meet their commitment by not being a no-show and by arriving on time for their visits. Putting it on paper and signing your name brings home the importance of what may seem like a little volunteer job. It also forces those coordinating a program to distill the purpose and requirements into a paragraph.

Since then, I've discovered that many churches also ask ushers, Sunday school teachers, and coffee hour coordinators to sign an agreement to serve, usually for one-year renewable terms. It helps solidify the commitment.

Training. For six weeks, the senior center provided new volunteers with role-playing exercises, question-and-answer sessions, and insights into the typical problems of the elderly. It felt great to be prepared.

Again, many churches utilize the same approach. In training sessions, Sunday school teachers role-play how to handle the disruptive child. Ushers discuss how to handle late arrivers. Committee chairs role-play how to deal with the committee member who won't stop talking.

Follow-up. It helps to discuss the challenges and questions that come up as we minister to others. Quarterly follow-up meetings came in handy, like the time I told the group about my difficulties with leaving Sarah.

Just when it was time to say good-by to Sarah each week, she would suddenly open up and talk about her problems, often with tears in her eyes. But until then, she would be very difficult to talk to. So, not wanting to leave during a meaningful moment, I'd end up feeling manipulated into staying longer than we had arranged.

In the follow-up sessions, the other volunteers told me I *was* being manipulated. From then on, when Sarah opened up as I was preparing to leave, I felt comfortable saying, "Sarah, I'd like to stay and talk, but I have to leave for another appointment." And I left. After that, Sarah opened up before the end of my visit.

Laity burnout is a serious problem for the church in this age of superbusy people; witness my hasty, unannounced departure from Resurrection Church. But by implementing some of the principles I learned the hard way, we can do much to avoid it.